POLISH POETRY
OF THE LAST TWO DECADES
OF COMMUNIST RULE

Spoiling Cannibals' Fun

Edited and with Translations by
Stanisław Barańczak and Clare Cavanagh

With a Foreword by Helen Vendler

NORTHWESTERN UNIVERSITY PRESS
Evanston, Illinois

Northwestern University Press
Evanston, Illinois 60201

Copyright © 1991 by Northwestern University Press
All rights reserved. Published 1991
Printed in the United States of America

First Printing, 1991

ISBN: 0-8101-0968-9 (cloth)
       0-8101-0982-4 (paper)

This volume was funded in part through the generosity of the National
Endowment for the Arts.

Library of Congress Cataloging-in-Publication Data

Polish poetry of the last two decades of communist rule : spoiling
    cannibals' fun / edited and with translations by Stanisław Barańczak
    and Clare Cavanagh ; with a foreword by Helen Vendler.
        p.   cm.
    Translated from Polish.
    Includes index.
    ISBN 0-8101-0968-9 (alk. paper). — ISBN 0-8101-0982-4 (pbk.)
    1. Polish poetry—20th century—Translations into English.
    I. Barańczak, Stanisław, 1946–   . II. Cavanagh, Clare.
    PG7445.E3P64   1991
    891.8'51708—dc20   91-3253
                                                                           CIP

The paper used in this publication meets the minimum requirements of
American National Standard for Information Sciences—Permanence of
Paper for Printed Library Materials, ANSI Z39.48-1984.

CONTENTS

ACKNOWLEDGMENTS

THE POETRY of Mieczysław Jastrun, Adam Ważyk, Jan Twardowski, Anna Kamieńska, Julia Hartwig, Tadeusz Różewicz, Artur Międzyrzecki, Jerzy Ficowski, Wiktor Woroszylski, Tadeusz Nowak, Urszula Kozioł, Jan Prokop, Leszek A. Moczulski, Ewa Lipska, Julian Kornhauser, Piotr Sommer, Tomasz Jastrun, Jan Polkowski, and Bronisław Maj appears by permission of Agencja Autorska, Warsaw. The poetry of Witold Wirpsza appears by permission of Leszek Szaruga. All other work appears by permission of the authors. The editors deeply regret that the present owner of the rights of the late Miron Białoszewski, Leszek Soliński, has refused to give his permission to publish the seventeen poems by Białoszewski that had originally been selected for inclusion in this anthology.

Some of the poems in this volume have been previously published in English translation and are reprinted by permission of the following.

Cross Currents: A Yearbook of Central European Culture: Zbigniew Herbert, "The Adventures of Mr. Cogito with Music"; Wisława Szymborska, "An Opinion on the Question of Pornography," "Writing a Résumé," "On Death, without Exaggeration," "Surplus," "The People on the Bridge"; Adam Zagajewski, "Flag," "Thorns," "Brevier."

Manhattan Review: Julia Hartwig, "Toward the End," "Before Dawn"; Ryszard Krynicki, "I Am Not Worthy," "Suddenly," "So What If," "The Wall"; Bronisław Maj, "These are strong, calm words . . . ," "Rain outside a window . . ."; Artur Międzyrzecki, "The Golden Age," "They," "29-77-02"; Jan Polkowski, "Among Us, the Unclean Ones," "Though Mortal, I Desired You"; Wisława Szymborska, "Stage Fright," "View with a Grain of Sand," "Plotting with the Dead"; Wiktor Woroszylski, " 'In this slough becoming stone . . . ,' " "What a Poem Is Allowed."

New York Review of Books: Zbigniew Herbert, "Report from a Besieged City," "Transformations of Livy."

Partisan Review: Julia Hartwig, "What Can They," "Above Us"; Ryszard Krynicki, "Socialist Realism," "You're Free," "A Stop," "Facing the Wall"; Bronisław Maj, "Who will bear witness to these times? . . . ," "This city died. Blue streetcars moan . . ."; Artur Międzyrzecki, "Fate the Clerk Lays Down a New Set of Bylaws," "The War of Nerves"; Jan Polkowski, "Hymn," "My Sweet Motherland"; Wisława Szymborska, "Our Ancestors'

Short Lives," "In Broad Daylight," "A Tale Begun"; Wiktor Woroszylski, "Fascist Nations," "Indictment," "The Padlock Speaks."

Ploughshares: Ryszard Krynicki, "The Answer," "The Heart," "I'll Remember That," "If It Comes to Pass."

Seneca Review: Jerzy Ficowski, "Ex-Jewish Things"; Tadeusz Nowak, "Psalm with No Answer"; Jan Prokop, "Song of a Crust of Bread ..."; Piotr Sommer, "Indiscretions"; Wisława Szymborska, "Clothes," "Into the Ark," "Possibilities."

Studium Papers: Wisława Szymborska, "Children of Our Age," "The Century's Decline."

Translation: Ernest Bryll, "Soot"; Jerzy Ficowski, "How to Spoil Cannibals' Fun"; Julia Hartwig, "Who Says"; Anna Kamieńska, "Funny"; Mieczysław Jastrun, "Mantegna's Christ"; Tomasz Jastrun, "Smoke"; Julian Kornhauser, "Barricade"; Ryszard Krynicki, "A New Day"; Ewa Lipska, "From the Gulf Stream of Sleep"; Bronisław Maj, "It takes just a few minutes ..."; Artur Międzyrzecki, "The Reason of Existence"; Leszek A. Moczulski, "Report"; Tadeusz Nowak, "Pastoral Psalm"; Jan Polkowski, "The Restaurant 'Arcadia,' Central Square, Nowa Huta"; Jan Prokop, "Song of Four-Egg Enriched Ribbon Noodles"; Tadeusz Różewicz, "The poet grows weaker .."; Piotr Sommer, "Medicine"; Wisława Szymborska, "The Great Man's House"; Jan Twardowski, "The Jesus of Nonbelievers"; Adam Ważyk, "The Offspring of Heraclitus"; Witold Wirpsza, "Mendacity"; Wiktor Woroszylski, "Philately."

TriQuarterly, a publication of Northwestern University: Julia Hartwig, "In Your Eyes," "But Of Course"; Ryszard Krynicki, "I Can't Help You," "Yes, She Says," "From a Window," "Do Not Want to Die for Us," "Sleep Well"; Bronisław Maj, "The world: whole and indivisible ..."; Artur Międzyrzecki, "At the Cave," "What Does the Political Scientist Know"; Wisława Szymborska, "Archaeology," "Hitler's First Photograph," "Funeral"; Wiktor Woroszylski, "Roommates."

Stanisław Barańczak, *Selected Poems: The Weight of the Body* (TriQuarterly/Another Chicago Press): "The Three Magi," "Along with the Dust," "To Grażyna," "Don't Use the Word 'Exile,' " "A Second Nature," "After Gloria Was Gone," "Setting a Hand Brake."

Zbigniew Herbert, *Report from the Besieged City* (Ecco Press): "Mr. Cogito's Soul," "Mr. Cogito—the Return," "Mr. Cogito and the Imagination," "Mr. Cogito on Virtue," "The Divine Claudius," "The Monster of Mr. Cogito," "Damastes (Also Known as Procrustes) Speaks," "The Power of Taste."

Ryszard Krynicki, *Citizen R. K. Does Not Live* (Mr. Cogito Press): "The Heart," "Rose," "Almost All," "If It Comes to Pass," "I Don't

Know," "The Answer," "I'll Remember That," "A New Day," "On the Eve."

Czesław Miłosz, *The Collected Poems, 1931-1987* (Ecco Press): "A Task," "Calling to Order," "Temptation," "Idea," "A Poetic State," "Distance," "Bypassing Rue Descartes," "Rivers," "Preparation," "Theodicy," "Poet at Seventy," "A Confession," "How It Should Be in Heaven," "Caffé Greco," "And Yet the Books," "1945."

Adam Zagajewski, *Tremor* (Farrar, Straus and Giroux): "Fire," "Iron," "The Trial," "A Polish Dictionary," "He Acts," "Lightning," "My Masters," "To Go to Lvov." Translation copyright © 1985 by Farrar, Straus & Giroux, Inc. Reprinted by permission of Farrar, Straus and Giroux, Inc.

FOREWORD

THE EXTRAORDINARY title of this anthology, announcing the end of Communist rule in Poland, at the same time confirms the persistence of art under that rule. The critic Walter Benjamin, accusing the art of the past of guilt by its association with oppressive cultural forces, wrote a famous aphorism declaring that every document of culture is also a document of barbarism. But when rule itself, as in Poland, becomes hostile to art, then culture goes underground, and the documents of culture exist in an adversarial relation to the sphere of power, rather than in collusion with it. Such documents take on the oblique nature of "the literature of the drawer"—literature that cannot be published in officially approved journals; but they also take on the lurid glow of pieces of criminal evidence, for which their authors can be—and often have been—jailed, exiled, or executed. In the catacombs of apartments under surveillance, in the hasty exchange of Xeroxes, in smuggled packets from prison, in defiantly published underground magazines, many of the poems printed here had their earlier covert existence. The gradual collapse of Communist rule between 1970 and 1989 (traced by Stanisław Barańczak in his Introduction to this volume) increasingly led to the uncensored publication of poetry. These poems, then, remain as memorials to an epoch that has ended, and to styles evolved in desperate response to an officially commanded hypocrisy or silence.

Any anthology of poetry from abroad offers the American reader new poets who arrest, charm, and provoke the mind, and this volume is no exception. Some who turn these pages will already know the brilliant, sardonic, and disturbing poetry of Czesław Miłosz (winner of the Nobel Prize in Poetry in 1980), and the severe parabolic poetry of Zbigniew Herbert (alias Mr. Cogito). There can scarcely be a single American reader, though, who will not find among these authors a new favorite poet. For me, it was a woman writer now in her sixties, Wisława Szymborska. Here she is, in a poem referred to by Barańczak, ironically transmitting the opinion of bureaucrats who are as scandalized by free thought as if it were a form of pornography:

There's nothing more debauched than thinking.
This sort of wantonness runs wild like a wind-borne weed
on a plot laid out for daisies.

Nothing's sacred for those who think.
Calling things brazenly by name,
risqué analyses, salacious syntheses,
frenzied, rakish chases after the bare facts,
the filthy fingering of touchy subjects, . . .

>   ("An Opinion on the Question of Pornography")

Another memorable Szymborska poem reflects on the perennial sameness of tortures, limited in every epoch by the constricted repertoire of the body:

Nothing has changed.
Except perhaps the manners, ceremonies, dances.
The gesture of the hands shielding the head
has nonetheless remained the same.
The body writhes, jerks, and tugs,
falls to the ground when shoved, pulls up its knees,
bruises, swells, drools, and bleeds.

>   ("Tortures")

For some readers, the striking new poet discovered here will be the co-editor himself, who was, before his arrival in the United States, one of the leading Polish dissidents. His years in Poland are commemorated by several poems, one of them a grim modern version of the visit of the Magi. As Barańczak opens his door on three visitors—policemen who have come to arrest him—he sees, we might say, the Muses of this volume, the Muses we could name Threat, Enjoinder, and Punishment. They wear their banal everyday faces, but they bear, even if unconsciously, gifts of ironic homage:

They will probably come just after the New Year. . . .
Three men. In one of them you'll recognize
with sheepish amazement (isn't this a small
world) your schoolmate of years ago.
Since that time he'll hardly have changed,
only grown a mustache,
perhaps gained a little weight.
They'll enter. The gold of their watches will glitter (isn't
this a gray dawn), the smoke from their cigarettes
will fill the room with a fragrance like incense.
All that's missing is myrrh, you'll think half-consciously—
while with your heel you're shoving under the couch the book they
        mustn't find—
what is this myrrh, anyway,

you'd have to finally look it up
someday. You'll come
with us, sir. You'll go
with them. Isn't this a white snow.
Isn't this a black Fiat.
Wasn't this a vast world.

("The Three Magi")

For still other readers, the new poet found in these pages may be
the rhapsodic Adam Zagajewski of "To Go to Lvov." Or it may be Ewa
Lipska, who articulates the resistance that "ordinary people," depressed by
her poetry, offer her in their questions at a poetry reading:

You don't have any hope?
You frighten us.
Why a black sky
or time shot down?
An empty hand, a hat that floats across the sea?
Why a wedding dress
with a funeral wreath?
Hospital halls
instead of garden paths?
Why not the future? Why the past?
Do you believe? You don't believe?
You frighten us.
We run from you.

("Questions at a Poetry Reading")

Though such a poem may spring from the Polish situation, it rings true in
other contexts. Many readers back away, in every country, from the
revealed face of the actual. "Humankind," as Eliot wrote, "cannot bear
very much reality." These Polish poets, no less than others elsewhere,
undergo repudiation by their audience (the very people they write to and
for). The voice crying in the wilderness often seems the central voice of
this book.

The individual poets in this collection have been translated, by sev-
eral hands, into an English always readable, often inspired. Each poem
included is a "real" poem, by which I mean that there shine in it those
qualities of imagination, concision, and architectonic firmness that one
finds in convincing lyrics. Much, of course, is missing: the intertextual lyric
references that must animate these poems in their original language; the
rhymes and rhythms that make lyric musical, the shades of diction serving
to summon up religious or political discourses ineluctably fixed in the

minds of the original audience for these poems (as Barańczak notes). Still, much remains. These voices, taken together, rise into a chorus of formidably ironic commentary. This chorus comments painfully and austerely not only on life lived under totalitarian censorship and punishment but also on life lived under the usual distractions and self-deceptions of the modern world.

Though it would be a mistake to read these poems solely in their Polish context, they will undoubtedly—in this moment of historical rupture—be read first of all as poems of witness to their cultural moment. They give anguishing testimony of what it is to live in an atmosphere in which everyone knows that anyone can have his or her will broken, that hypocrisy is the order of the day, that the mental sphere itself is invaded by the absence of personal freedom, and that the function of art is clouded by its political helplessness. Nonetheless, the poems give ingenious testimony as well to the way the imagination bursts out even in these unpropitious circumstances (however propitious they may be in another, terrifying, sense). They reveal how, under totalitarian censorship, the necessary resort of poetry to double meaning, allegory, displaced symbolism, covert voicing, and so on, confirms the inventive drive of lyric toward the truth, no matter in how oblique a way. The formal variety here is enormously interesting; one hardly knew so many sly amusements were possible to the lyric voice in its satirical manifestation, nor how much of Poland's politically rebellious past could be inserted into the modern situation in heartfelt and passionate terms. A reader of the Polish originals could tell accurately the degree to which the language of postwar Poland has made its way into the verse collected by Barańczak and Clare Cavanagh; but even in translation one hears echoes of the language-field of contemporary Poland—the wooden language of the Communist state, street slang, prayer, coded dissident discourse, literary allusion.

What will Polish poets do without the Communist system to rebel against? And how many assumptions of the system have invisibly entered the conceptual equipment of the younger, Communist-raised poets? And where will new Polish poets locate political good and evil? In an essay printed in his collection *Solidarity, Solitude* (Ecco Press, 1990), Adam Zagajewski says of antitotalitarianism that it depended "on placing all the world's evil in one place: totalitarianism. . . . They, the totalitarians, are evil. We are good and innocent. . . . They keep us enslaved, we oppose them." Such a view cannot long be held by a responsible poet. Zagajewski continues,

Antitotalitarianism at its best and noblest tempts me with unreality, the unreality of the good. . . . But I am incapable of being just pure and just good. I know that I live in the throes of contradictions, in constant tension, ambiguity. . . . I want to think against myself, against us, and not just against *them*. (pp. 69–70)

This necessary complexity of post-Communist imaginative vision offers a program for new Polish poetry. The Mr. Cogitos of Poland will not lack for things to write about with respect to their own past and future; and the old and distinguished resources of the Polish literary tradition, from folk ballads to historical epics, will surely not fail them. As this collection proves, they have an astonishingly gifted set of forebears to live up to.

Helen Vendler

INTRODUCTION

OF THE THREE words that form the subtitle of this anthology (the phrase itself has been borrowed from one of the poems translated here), each can be accused of satirical overkill. To begin with, the rulers of Communist Poland between 1970 and 1989 were not exactly cannibals. Even though many of them were directly or indirectly responsible for the loss of human lives or quite ruthless persecution, the essence of the last two decades of Poland's version of totalitarianism seems to lie not so much in an exceptional degree of brutality as in an exceptional degree of incompetence on the part of the country's administrators and of shabbiness in the rapidly declining system. Second, no one in his or her right mind would believe that, even for power-hungry Communist apparatchiks, ruling over a nation so clearly set against them might have been any kind of "fun." And third, it would also be an inexcusable exaggeration on the part of a presumptuous poet or an overly enthusiastic poetry fan to maintain seriously that poetry in our times does indeed, if only in certain parts of the world, represent a tangible power to be reckoned with. If poetry can sometimes be visualized as a stick poked in History's wheel, it is, by definition, a stick never sturdy enough actually to stop the chariot or even to slow down its relentless movement, thus genuinely "spoiling" the pleasure it takes in crushing nations and individual lives.

And yet, if there was any country during the past twenty years where poets were able to "spoil cannibals' fun" at least to some extent, it was precisely Poland.

By saying this, I am by no means trying to give Polish poetry credit for directly influencing the course of political events in the seventies and eighties. In fact, I am not even talking about "political poetry," whatever this vague term might mean. What I do have in mind is, rather, that Polish poetry of the last two decades offered an astonishingly wide array of individual human responses to the faceless inhumanity of state oppression and a hopeless future—and, by virtue of this alone, has proved something that modern man is often prone to doubt. It has proved that in today's world there are still large areas of human experience that only poetry can explore and put into words.

It cannot be emphasized enough that this anthology is not restricted to directly political themes, much less to partisan approaches of any kind.

1

On the contrary, it is precisely the anthology's thematic variety and the pluralistic coexistence of different outlooks that may engage, we hope, the reader's interest. The sheer number of religious poems included here, for example, may surprise someone who expects that poets of the times of turmoil will restrict themselves to recording solely the turmoil of the times. And yet, it is impossible to detach even what appear to be the most universal and apolitical among these poems—yes, even the purely religious ones—from the background of recent history. After all, it cannot be a matter of pure chance that in Poland the seventies and eighties form an epoch as abundant in earth-shaking political events as it was rich in brilliant poetic achievements. This era began with a workers' rebellion in December 1970 (or, more exactly, with the earlier protests of intellectuals and students in March 1968) and continued through another wave of social unrest in June 1976. This was followed, in turn, by a long series of unprecedented events: the creation of human rights groups such as KOR (Workers' Defense Committee) and a wide network of uncensored publishing in 1976; the emergence of Solidarity in August 1980; its tragic setback caused by the imposition of martial law at the end of 1981; its prolonged underground existence; and its final victory at the polls in the summer of 1989, as Poland moved from Soviet-style communism to parliamentary democracy and a market economy.

This unique historical experience coincided with a resurgence of Polish poetry. It was precisely during the period ushered in by the ill-fated rebellions of intellectuals in 1968 and workers in 1970 that many older poets entered, as it were, a second youth, writing their best work to date; at the same time, a generation of younger poets (the so-called New Wave or Generation of '68) rapidly gained recognition. A strong current of poetry of social protest and ethical concerns emerged and grew alongside new manifestations of existential or metaphysical lyricism. As a result, the generally gloomy and oppressive atmosphere of the seventies and eighties (with the exception of sixteen months of Solidarity's open existence between August 1980 and December 1981) produced, ironically, a large number of poetic works of historic significance and universal appeal.

It is an odd feeling to realize that an epoch has ended and that our own lives up to now already belong to a certain closed period, a recognizable segment of history. The Communist phase in the history of Eastern Europe, which seemed endless while it dragged on, turned out, to everybody's astonishment, to be nothing more than that—a phase, a distinct unit of the historical process which we now hope to have happily left behind us. Communism's collapse was so sudden and complete that it is easy to forget today what life in the jaws of the totalitarian Leviathan was like. At the same time, a look back from today's vantage point makes it possible to realize the enormous dimensions of the changes that took place in the consciousness of the Polish people during the turbulent events of the seventies and eighties. Specifically, all that has happened in the sociopolitical domain since August 1980 has contributed to one of the most crucial experiences in the history of the Polish nation. The sudden awakening of the society's most vital and authentic forces in 1980 and then, sixteen months later, the regime's attempt to crush those forces by declaring war against that society have created an unprecedented situation. Both Polish society as a whole and each of its individual members were confronted with a set of new dilemmas, ranging from the practical tactics of everyday survival to profound questions of an ethical and, I would not hesitate to say, even metaphysical nature. Each of these dilemmas demanded a resolution if one was to find some sense in an apparently senseless existence, some hope in an apparently hopeless predicament. And, as we can imagine, none of these dilemmas could easily be resolved then.

I have just said that it was the sociopolitical situation itself that made people face those dilemmas. But, of course, things are usually not that simple. As a rule, there is an intermediary between society's experience and the individual's psyche—a kind of go-between that can be called culture. If not for that, the outer world of facts and events and the inner world of feelings and thoughts would resemble two interlocutors speaking different languages with no way to communicate. It is precisely culture that serves as an interpreter—an interpreter who helps us to understand what reality tells us and what it asks us about, and who, at the same time, helps us to formulate our own questions and responses in a comprehensible language of symbols.

Within culture, perhaps the most apt interpreter of this kind is poetry. I have in mind not only the specifically Polish cultural tradition, in which the privileged role of poetry has been constant since the time of the great Romantics. My point is also more general: I think it might be said that lyric poetry—which by its very nature is the voice of the individual—is the first to react whenever culture faces the task of "translating" the common experience of society into the language of individual sensation; poetry is the quickest to put into words those questions that History poses to the individual human life and that human life poses to History.

No wonder, then, that in Poland the past two decades, and particularly the eighties, witnessed a genuine explosion of lyric poetry writing, which came to dominate other literary genres. (Instead of Poland, we should speak rather of the larger realm of Polish writing: one of the most fascinating features of recent Polish literary life has been the rapid disappearance of the traditional borderline dividing Poland-based and émigré literatures and communities of writers. The greatest presence in Polish poetry of this period, Czesław Miłosz, is so prominently represented in this anthology precisely because his émigré voice is listened to so intently in Poland.) It is worth noting that in these other, nonlyric genres the predominant trends seemed to stem from a feeling—overtly expressed or not—of literature's insufficiency in confrontation with reality. The novel, for instance, turned more and more often into a sort of extended essay or reportage, the short story was more and more often replaced by something like an expanded entry from the writer's diary. In contrast, Polish lyric poetry clearly flourished, and it did so even in its generically strictest, that is to say, most typically lyric, forms. The same sense of overwhelming reality that inhibited the novelists seemed to spur the creativity of the poets. Of course, this does not necessarily mean that the results of this creativity were always first-rate: as is only natural, alongside the peaks of great achievements there were also valleys of mediocrity, and even pits of graphomania. Be that as it may, Poland between 1970 and 1989 could rightly be described as a country where poetry was needed. Poetry was read there—and not only read but also smuggled from abroad or printed underground, which could (especially in the first years of martial law) involve harsh consequences for the smuggler, printer, editor, distributor, or even reader of such material. The fact that so many people were willing to risk those consequences provides a fairly reliable indication that in Poland poetry was a means of expression from which much was expected and which, to all intents and purposes, was able to satisfy these expectations.

The existence of the so-called second and third network of publication, just mentioned in passing, was of crucial importance as far as the reader's trust in poetry was concerned. Since the mid-seventies, when a significant number of Poland-based authors had begun to publish their work in émigré presses and when, simultaneously, a network of underground domestic publishing houses was being formed, Polish literary life was based on the coexistence of three forms of publication and circulation: the official one, which was subject to censorship, and two uncensored ones, the émigré and the underground systems, which were technically illegal but prospered in spite of all searches and confiscations. The consequences for literature of this sort of pluralism were already tremendous by the early eighties. On the one hand, this state of affairs created a welcome alternative for the writer who did not feel like cutting deals with the censor. It even indirectly mollified the censors' policies, by forcing them to realize that too much red pencil could result in the author's withdrawing his or her book from the official publishing house and offering the manuscript to an émigré or underground publisher. On the other hand, this situation also created a heightened sense of responsibility. Since the censored network's monopoly had been broken and outlets were available for publishing maverick thoughts and controversial opinions, no writer could claim any longer that he "had to" suppress or distort the truth in his work because he had to make peace with the censor. It does not mean that at any time before 1989 Poland actually dispensed with censorship (the formal elimination of that institution occurred only in the spring of 1990); it means, rather, that many Polish writers managed to dispense with self-censorship. In other words, the reader of the eighties had every right to expect that the writers wrote as they did not in order to deceive the censor but for their own artistic purposes.

There is no need to stress how profoundly this general change in expectations affected literary language and style. If we focus on poetry, where the problem of language and style is of utmost importance, we can see that this change has completely remodeled the nature and significance of certain devices and approaches that had traditionally been considered characteristic of modern Polish poetry.

Take the case of irony. In the officially published poetry of the late 1950s, 1960s, and even part of the 1970s, irony functioned chiefly as a weapon of self-defense, effective mainly because of its clever indirection. Considered as both a literary device and a more general method of communication, irony can be defined as a way of speaking in which three persons are involved but only two of them are partners in the dialogue: the "ironist" speaks in front of two "listeners," only one of whom is able to understand his indirect message, while the other, irony-deaf, becomes the "victim" of irony. Now if we assume that "the ironist" is the poet, "the listener" is his intelligent reader, and the "victim" of irony is some otherwise powerful bully (for example, the regime), it will be easy to understand the reasons behind the extensive use of irony in poetry that was subject to censorship. Does that mean that irony completely evaporated from the uncensored poetry of the 1980s? Of course not, but it was used for different purposes. Its inherent indirectness was no longer needed to fool the censor, but it continued to play a very important role as a means of intensifying and complicating a poem's meanings.

The issue of irony is especially significant for our remarks on Polish poetry in the 1980s, since irony's absence or presence is the chief indicator that helps us to distinguish certain basic trends here. As early as 1982 I had the opportunity to review the first underground anthology of the "poetry of the state of war" (*Poezja stanu wojennego*, a slim book published in London but written and edited in Poland), and it struck me then that the apparent variety of poetic approaches in that collection came down, in fact, to just two basic methods connected with two different concepts of a lyric speaker (if we omit the instances of anonymous literary folklore, which form a third, sociologically and aesthetically different, approach). We can call these two basic concepts the perspective of the Single Observer and the perspective of the Romantic Visionary. The Single Observer's point of view was concrete and specific: it consisted of a circle of observations within the reach of a single participant or witness of events, a person like thousands of others but at the same time an individual burdened with a particular fate and a unique experience. What was especially striking here was the speaker's emotional restraint: confronted with a historical cataclysm, he or she reacted by trying to convey a rigorously faithful account not so much of personal feelings as of external reality. However, insofar as the essence of that reality was its paradoxicality or even downright absurdity, this kind of reaction did not preclude the strong presence of irony.

In contrast, irony was virtually absent from the perspective of the Romantic Visionary, who assumed a more panoramic point of view while also becoming a less individualized figure. Here, the first person singular changed to plural; not the individual but "we," the people, were the lyrical hero of the poem. Appropriately, the specific, limited space within which the Single Observer was usually located was replaced by a vast, bird's-eye view of the entire country. The poem's temporal span was even more laden with philosophical consequences: instead of focusing on a particular moment, the observation embraced, as it were, centuries of Polish history. Not the uniqueness of experience but its opposite, the cyclic repetition of the same experiences throughout history, drew the attention of the poet: General Jaruzelski's war against the Polish people was seen as nothing more, or less, than another link in a long chain of crushed insurrections and abolished reforms. Accordingly, traditional, mostly Romantic, stylistic conventions were almost automatically unearthed and revived.

We must not overlook the fundamental philosophical difference between these two approaches. The poetry of Romantic vision, by emphasizing the cyclical nature of History, grudgingly acknowledged the presence of some superior sense even in History's most foolish vagaries. Rebelling against the "eternal Polish fate," such poetry nonetheless admitted that something like an eternal, unchangeable Polish fate did exist. Only a short step remained to catastrophic, dead-end despair. The Single Observer, on the other hand, reasoned in an entirely different way. In his view, what had happened since the imposition of martial law on 13 December 1981 was the total opposite of logic—it was, first and foremost, absurd. Romantic pathos and historical analogies could only dim that truth; in the view of the Single Observer, it was enough for a poet simply to reflect ironically the basic paradoxes and contradictions of what was going on in order to reveal reality's fundamental absurdity and thus to counter, as far as poetry could, its crushing impact.

What I am talking about are the first manifestations of "post-December" poetry—the first poetic reactions to the reality of the "state of war." But I think my diagnosis of 1982 has been fully confirmed by the further developments of Polish poetry in the 1980s. The basic opposition between two perspectives, that of the Romantic Visionary and that of the Single Observer, resurfaced time and again and continued to express a significant philosophical and aesthetic divergence. If we look, for instance, at one important underground publication, at Jarosław Marek Rymkiewicz's collection *Mandelstam Street* (*Ulica Mandelsztama*, 1983), we are almost forced to view these poems as embodiments of a typically Romantic vision, a vision accepted in dead seriousness, with all the consequences it entails. When we read this volume we have every reason to take the author's assertions at face value: he, or at least his lyric speaker, really means it when he builds in his poems a sort of uninterrupted continuity of historical times and, in consequence, draws strict analogies between Poland under Jaruzelski and Poland under the czarist or Nazi oppressors. But this emphasis on the unchangeability of the "Polish fate" forces Rymkiewicz to resort continually to Romantic stylization, with all its dangerous excesses in pathos and loftiness. Such a vehement turn toward Romantic vision and style is an especially ironic development in this particular case, since in the 1960s and 1970s the same Rymkiewicz had made himself known as a programmatic neoclassicist, cosmopolitan rather than nationalistic, and ironically restrained rather than overly emotional. It is interesting to compare this sudden metamorphosis with the reverse processes taking place in the works of other poets. Ernest Bryll, for instance, who in the 1960s and 1970s had become a famous albeit controversial figure thanks to poems marked by an extremely Romantic vision and nationalistic themes, seemed in his later poetry (published underground and also collected in the volume *Advent* that came out in London) to have shifted his focus toward a scrupulous observation of everyday reality.

One must admit that the return to the Romantic tradition has found several talented exponents in recent Polish poetry: besides Rymkiewicz, an especially important and popular example is the younger poet Tomasz Jastrun. In my opinion, however, the greatest achievements of Polish poetry in the eighties are tied to the anti-Romantic, ironic, and specific perspective of the Single Observer. The simplest—but also one of the freshest and most effective—method of creating such poetry is, as I said before, the straightforward registration of facts and realistic details without any outside commentary: in this way, reality itself unmasks its inherent absurdity. It is highly significant that such an accomplished poet as Wiktor

Woroszylski chooses the genre of a poetic diary—which seemingly confines itself to jotting down everyday observations—to give an account of his stay in an internment camp in 1981–82. The images of absurdity presented in his cycle "Diary of Internment" speak for themselves. This does not bar some of Woroszylski's poems from acquiring a more metaphorical and symbolic meaning. The poem entitled "The Belly of Barbara N.," for instance, is again based on fact—it portrays a real-life woman whose pregnancy did not make her exempt from internment during martial law—but the fact develops here into a bitterly ironic metaphor for the common fate of citizens in a totalitarian state.

Woroszylski's "Diary of Internment" was just one of the first reactions to the bewilderingly new situation of the "state of war." Throughout the eighties, an increasing number of poetic collections appeared that tried to employ, in a variety of ways, the perspective of the Single Observer and the mechanisms of irony while also working to develop a broader vision of a philosophical, historiological, aesthetic, or ethical nature. New collections of older poets such as Zbigniew Herbert, Wisława Szymborska, Julia Hartwig, Miron Białoszewski, or Artur Międzyrzecki; the collections of poets now in their forties such as Ewa Lipska, Ryszard Krynicki, or Adam Zagajewski; or the poetic publications of somewhat younger writers such as Jan Polkowski or Bronisław Maj are not merely outstanding achievements in their own right. They also give startling proof of how different individual visions can be.

Some of the poems that appeared in those collections were, to be sure, older than 1980; the specific context of the 1980s, however, gave them a new dimension. This is the case with, perhaps more than any other poet, Zbigniew Herbert, whose 1983 collection *Report from the Besieged City (Raport z oblężonego miasta)* deserves to be called the greatest poetic sensation of the decade. The poems collected in this volume, which Herbert published, for the first time in his career, with an émigré publishing house, range from two poems from the late 1950s (suppressed by the censor for all those years) to poems written under and about martial law. Within Herbert's output, *Report* is a publication of special, almost revelatory significance. While continuing the previous thematic and stylistic lines of his work, it also shows him in a new light: not as a stoical neoclassicist, as many critics had tended to view him, but as a profoundly ambivalent and tragic poet torn between two sets of antinomic values: between the past and the present, the Western heritage and Poland's specificity, myth and history, culture and tangible experience. The first of these sets of values is the heritage from which we have been dispossessed but to which we lay claim; the second is the lot which has befallen us regardless of our will but which cannot simply be dismissed or rejected. Therefore Herbert's lyric persona, Mr. Cogito, is always torn in two, suspended between opposing values—but he finds solution and solace in the irony that helps him to preserve the necessary distance from his own misery. It is especially important to note that irony in Herbert does not preclude a moralistic stance, the call to maintain an "upright attitude," that is, to remain faithful to imponderable principles. This is especially clear in the famous poem "The Power of Taste," in which the author's heroic independence during the Stalinist years is ironically depreciated only to emerge finally as a norm of behavior to which he adheres quite seriously. An even more famous poem in the same collection, the title poem, refers unequivocally to the moral dilemmas of the "state of war" in Poland. An apparently hopeless defense of the "besieged city" of humanistic values becomes here, despite or perhaps precisely because of its hopelessness, a mission that must not be abandoned under any circumstances.

This complex blend of irony and moralism, which has been Herbert's hallmark for many years, also characterizes the creative method of the premier Polish woman poet, Wisława Szymborska. Szymborska's volume *The People on the Bridge* (*Ludzie na moście*), published in 1986 as her first collection in ten years, is undoubtedly the best book so far in her long and rich career, as well as one of the poetic highlights of the 1980s. Szymborska has never been a political poet in a strict sense—thus her book could emerge unscathed from a censored publishing house—but no one will fail to recognize the indirect political significance of her tireless defense of the individual and the ridicule of any dogmatic authority that continuously informs her poetry. What strikes the reader of the twenty-two brilliant poems that make up *The People on the Bridge* is that each of them, all their paradoxicality and ironic wit notwithstanding, relates closely to the experiences and reflections of the common man, of the average thinking individual. Szymborska's method is to take an element of everyday experience and refract it through a prism of a specific narrative or stylistic device so that reality's absurdity or senselessness compromises itself, as it were. A dazzling example of this indirect technique is her seemingly hilarious—but also very sad—poem "An Opinion on the Question of Pornography." On its surface the poem seems to allude to the endless debates on whether to legalize pornography, which, for lack of more interesting topics, filled the pages of the censored press in Poland throughout the eighties. But what Szymborska does with this material goes much further. She puts "an opinion on the question of pornography" into the mouth of an imagined supporter of "law and order" who quite rightly maintains that pornography *stricto sensu* is far less subversive than thinking as such. After the initial orgy of comical double entendres and sexual allusions, the poem's ending rings a deliberately sobering note: the anonymous speaker unwittingly reveals that the reality of "law and order" he defends is the reality of a totalitarian country where the very act of thinking entails fear of police persecution.

Long considered the most outstanding among Poland's numerous women poets, in recent decades Szymborska has found a worthy competitor in Julia Hartwig. Hartwig's rapid creative growth during the eighties has secured her a prominent place in contemporary Polish poetry. The publication of her most recent collection, *Relations (Obcowanie)* in 1987, in particular, marked a breakthrough in her career. This book shows Hartwig as a poet close to both Herbert and Szymborska in her fundamental conviction of the inevitable imperfection of the human being. In spite of all the ideologies bent on perfecting mankind, the individual's destiny—the destiny of a representative of a species burdened with consciousness and its inseparable companions, guilt and doubt—is a constant "not measuring up to" this or that ideal, an incompleteness, undefinability, inability to belong in the unthinking and therefore safe worlds of both ahistoric Nature and historic Utopia. However, since Being as such is imperfect too, Hartwig also views mankind's imperfection as a privilege: only an imperfect creature can provide trustworthy testimony about the imperfection of Being. The usual modus operandi of Hartwig's poetry is, therefore, her tracing of the various forms of the individual's incompleteness, inner inconsistency, "duality." Yet this basically philosophical set of questions and tasks is never left hanging in the sterile air of abstraction; on the contrary, it gains its poetic force precisely by being rooted in the specific experience of a given place and time—Poland in the seventies and eighties.

Artur Międzyrzecki's *War of Nerves (Wojna nerwów,* 1983) and Miron Białoszewski's *Oho* (1985) are two other examples of books that came out through the censored publishing network but, despite certain deletions, managed to remain highly convincing lyrical accounts of contemporary Polish reality. They are two very different accounts, to be sure. For Międzyrzecki, the central problem in the phenomenon of the "state of war" is the clash between brute force and the values represented by culture. He views it stoically as a perennial and universal conflict that permeates centuries of human civilization: it is not a duel that can be resolved once and for all but, rather, an endless "war of nerves" in which only a moral victory can be won. The uncertainty of this kind of victory forces Międzyrzecki, not unlike Herbert, to realize that under the present circumstances the worst mistake that the poet-moralist could make would be to promise his or her readers too much, to delude them with too much hope. The only hope the poet can offer is a belief in the continuity of values represented by culture and an awareness of the unpredictability of human history.

Białoszewski expresses a similar belief in a highly idiosyncratic and much less direct manner.° His posthumous collection (he died in 1983), whose publication was one of the major events of aboveground literary life in the 1980s, is as unique as anything he ever wrote, but it also surpasses his earlier work in the unflinching precision with which he probes the fabric of society's life at a given historic moment. Among its other themes, *Oho*—a collection of poems, mini-narratives, and dramatic dialogues—is also a book on the everyday reality of martial law in Warsaw; and it is paradoxical that Białoszewski, long considered an extreme individualist and lyrical solipsist, emerges here as the author of arguably the most realistic and detailed literary portrayal of the "state of war" and its impact on Polish society. He does so in his own unorthodox way; instead of striking a sacrificial or catastrophic note, he creates a grotesque sequence, "Kitty Katty's Cabaret" ("Kabaret Kici Koci"). "The Cabaret" consists mostly of comical scenes and songs in which the main roles are played by a quartet of Warsaw old ladies with fanciful names like Kitty Katty, Sibyl of Grochów, Stressa, and Blessed Grandmaya from Vishnuville. Dividing their time between standing in lines, gossip, and oriental philosophy, the ladies witness and take part in various situations typical of the months before and after the imposition of martial law. Białoszewski reproduces with infallible accuracy and humor not only the external details of his characters' behavior but also the ways in which people's reactions are reflected in their everyday speech.

We return here, once again, to the problem of irony. By employing the device of the dialogue and the quasi-dramatic scene instead of lyrical confession, Białoszewski creates his own kind of ironic distance. This, in turn, enables him to see the reality of martial law without pathos or hysteria, to bring it down to earth. But precisely this concreteness, this assumption of the perspective of the man in the street, makes it possible for him, at the same time, to express a sense of solidarity with his characters and with the society they represent. Thus he appears in *Oho*, even more clearly than in his previous work, as a poet whose extremely individualistic stance coexists amazingly—but quite consistently—with his respectful, almost humble attitude toward anything that remains beyond the borders of the individual self, including the world of other people, with their hopes, disappointments, and miseries.

The question of how to reconcile poetry's natural individualism with human solidarity and respect for supraindividual values is, in fact, the single most pressing issue that Polish poetry faced during the last decades

° Much to the editors' regret, the seventeen poems of the late Miron Białoszewski that they had selected and translated for this anthology could not be included for copyright reasons. See the Acknowledgments.

of Communist rule. It was fascinating to observe how this dilemma was approached by various poets of the younger generation, such as Ryszard Krynicki, Adam Zagajewski, Ewa Lipska, Julian Kornhauser, Piotr Sommer, Jan Polkowski, or Bronisław Maj. Born in the 1940s and 1950s, most of these poets entered literary life in the wake of the political protests of 1968, 1970, or 1976, and all of them contributed greatly to the "social awakening" of Polish poetry in the early 1970s and after. The recent poetry of Krynicki, for instance, is an extreme manifestation of the individual self's humility in the face of commonly shared values and compassion for human suffering. This essentially Christian attitude goes along with a heightened sense of responsibility for the word. Krynicki goes so far as to equate a poem with a slogan chalked on a wall or a demonstrator's cry: like these, the poem must be as brief as possible, cleansed of unnecessary words, reduced to its bare semantic essence. Accordingly, most of Krynicki's recent poems, sometimes consisting of just two or three lines, structurally resemble the genres of aphorism or parable.

By contrast, the recent poetry of Zagajewski, the other of the two most outstanding representatives of the so-called Generation of '68, appears to be headed in a diametrically opposed direction. Like Krynicki, Zagajewski began his literary career as a poet, novelist, and essayist protesting against the omnipresent ideological lie of the system. In particular, in 1974 he stirred up one of the greatest controversies in postwar Polish culture by coauthoring, with Kornhauser, a book of criticism titled *The World Not Represented*, a sweeping assault on the noncommittal literature of the preceding decades. Yet the poetry he has written since 1981, though concerned for a while with the reality of the "state of war," has been far from expressing any clear-cut political tendency. Rather, these poems form a portrayal of an individual mind torn asunder by contradictory tendencies—by the moral obligation to speak on behalf of others as opposed to the necessity of remaining one's unique self. The poet's ironic and self-ironic consciousness never allows him to accept anything that is abstract, general, collectivist; ironic distance is used here as a defensive weapon against the leveling abstractness of ideologies and systems. But it is, by the same token, also necessary to take in the whole breathtaking *plurality* of the concrete, tangible world. In poems where the concept of plurality becomes predominant, such as "To Go to Lvov," Zagajewski moves in the opposite direction to Krynicki: while the latter's brief and concise utterances can be called poem-aphorisms, Zagajewski's rich, overflowing, almost baroque odes deserve the name of (to borrow a term from Miłosz) poem-tapestries. But these poems are not merely outbursts of rapture and admiration for the fundamental plurality of the world. Zagajewski realizes that this plurality also encompasses evil and injustice.

This becomes particularly evident when we encounter evil masquerading as History: witness Zagajewski's powerful poems about martial law in Poland, such as "Iron."

Yet even in such poems he remains an individualist whose ironic distance does not stand in opposition to his compassion and moralistic concern; on the contrary, it is exactly this ironic distance that gives him the chance to see reality's evil more clearly and soberly. And, in a sense, this paradoxical reconciliation between the extremes of individualism and moralism is, regardless of all the differences in approach and style, a unifying feature of whatever is most valuable in recent Polish poetry.

Stanisław Barańczak
September 1990

A Note on the Translations

Unless otherwise indicated, the translations are by Stanisław Barańczak and Clare Cavanagh. Barańczak has translated his own poems.

Mieczysław Jastrun

1903–83

Mantegna's Christ

MANTEGNA'S Christ, stretched on the ground,
With enormous foreshortened feet.
The epoch shows us its feet the same way,
Pierced, magnified, foreshortened by centuries,
The feet of a corpse, whom we, the living,
Try to revive with our breath and bathe in raining tears—
The feet of the Lazarus whom God became
To avoid dying in his awful glory.

Waiting in Line

NEWLYWEDS with white flowers
came out of the church and caught a cab their ears
still full of the organ's benediction
Here though there's noise and exhaust fumes
Women wrapped in sheepskins boots to their knees
teased hair beneath their scarves
broad-hipped wrinkled not from age
but from failed lives Housewives used
to scolding in lines scrounging for the food
that dark kitchens and tables are waiting for
And if they don't bring home meat the man gets mad
who's borne for hours the factory's brunt the rumble
of the conveyor belt the emptiness
after the night shift when the day begins
and sleep seeps through shaded windows into bed
Tomorrow is today and the way between days is narrow
So they've learned how to complain in voices sharp as razors
to elbow into lines to borrow kids for extra portions
Fertile at least Their hips remember the births

of boys grown tall and thin who snicker at the queuers
even at those who are mothers of life
They'll wait in this crush until the doors swing open
wide as a window on a sunny day.

Repatriate

AFTER TWELVE years he returned
gaunt awkward acting
excessively polite
What he tells beneath his breath
is light and darkness
we know it now
from books—but yesterday?
At the table he still has a kind of gaze
that's not his own that catches him
at every word in reddened eyelids
where those inhuman years
lie hidden
A repatriate from Vorkuta
I still see him
His eyes turned lifelessly
to the place from which the light does not return
Whatever you say about him
his half-open lips remain unsaid
His hands speak at the table by the oak tree
though his words define a form
that does not admit outsiders
that remains a prison shield
despite his return
As if he longed to enter swirling clouds
that are in fact no more.

Light from Another World

ONE LIFE has passed
I passed over what hurt the most
in silence
I forgot about the changes
they grew pale like stars at dawn
shining in leafless trees
Light from another world
embraced me

A hyacinth's keen scent
And nothing—like a stone thrown into water
nothing—like water turned to stone
frozen by the morning cold

One life has passed

I passed over silence in silence
I forgot
on this planet where it was so hard
to square endless otherness
with my own brief time

A steep staircase opened beneath me
leading to a tunnel underground
where letters
on the wall spelled
the saving phrase: "Way Out."

Adam Ważyk
1905–82

The Offspring of Heraclitus

WE BELIEVE neither in time's circle
nor in its spiraling mountain
the past is order
the future is contingency
A window is opened
through which nothing can be seen
we are given lips
that may not touch the same water twice
we are given hostile dreams
and experience
that speaks to us in a foreign tongue
we've grown used to its sound
and pick out the occasional phrase

A Sigh

AH I SO OFTEN wish to call up as before
sweltering noons and ruddy, puffy clouds
the greedy green, the glee of fruit
glances' liquor and the shred of silk
candles dripping on night's velveteen
the gleam of a woman's arm, the black of coal
suburban melancholy's mercury the roar
of gunshots laughter motors wrath
I wish and write and speak in vain
there are no metaphors there's just the taste of salt
no splendid colors just the heavy earth

The Loop

ON A FROZEN snowless January evening how awful
to get off the bus where it turns back from its last deserted stop
At the far end of the avenue dear Undine
with pale eyes and wide dry lips
you hunch and huddle in your sheepskin coat
You walk between the wooden huts and the housing projects
where it's frightening to hear footsteps or smell smoke
Here fires flare up quickly and aren't easy to put out
a frame shack flames up like a pagan pyre
out there somewhere someone's dancing, someone's singing, someone
    talks to God
but very far away while you scared stiff
count beneath your breath the bare familiar chestnut trees
clutch the tear-gas pistol in your pocket
and over gravel that squeaks like a tiny animal
run your hair streaming to your home

A Plan

IF I BELIEVED at all
I might beg God to spare me
from train passengers with heavy civil-servant stares
that waver between arrogance and fear
from paper-rustling poets
from aesthetes and expressionists
from the noun lifestyle the adjective postmodern
from the horrifying phrase nouvelle cuisine
and I'd have to make room in my litany
for those poor lady singers on TV
whose arms keep pumping some imaginary pump
the soccer kicks twelve feet above the goal
that sportscasters always call gorgeous
would-be movies
comedies done tongue in cheek
debates
would-be advertisements

Metal Export up in neon lights
would-be life
but regrettably I can't compose this litany
because I don't believe

A *Time without Prophets*

ALL THE PROPHETS had fallen silent
though it was not a time of silence
men made speeches at meetings
women shouted
at conferences on Sex and Politics

The keys that were looked for
were only in pockets and drawers
the doors that were knocked at
were just in offices and homes
there were no real journeys
voyages to the isles of bliss
just improvised substitute trips
that eased the burden of existence for a bit
day came like a thief in the night
only to one young couple
on the ninth floor of a high rise
who jumped up suddenly
to stifle the alarm clock's rattle

The sleepy woman was reaching for her robe
the man was shaving in the bathroom
with the door open
this made conjugal dialogue possible
and as long as they talked about ordinary things
everything was clear
meanwhile their images
naked as in Eden
etched on a rocket's wall
and launched into space

were hurtling who knows where
no answer was expected
for the next six hundred years
and none was expected later

January 1976

Czesław Miłosz
1911–

A Task

IN FEAR and trembling, I think I would fulfill my life
Only if I brought myself to make a public confession
Revealing a sham, my own and of my epoch:
We were permitted to shriek in the tongue of dwarfs and demons
But pure and generous words were forbidden
Under so stiff a penalty that whoever dared to pronounce one
Considered himself as a lost man.

Berkeley, 1970
Translated by Czesław Miłosz

Calling to Order

YOU COULD scream
Because mankind is mad.
But you, of all people, should not.

Out of what thin sand
And mud and slime
Out of what dogged splinters
Did you fashion your castle against the test of the sea,
And now it is touched by a wave.

What chaos
Received bounds, from here to there.
What abyss
Was seen and passed over in silence.
What fear
Of what you are.

It shows itself
But that is not it.
It is named

Yet remains nameless.
It is coming to be
But has not begun.

Your castle will topple
Into the wine-colored
Funereal sea,
She will assuage your pride.

Yet you knew how
To use next to nothing.
It is not a matter of wisdom
Or virtue.

So how can you condemn
The unreason of others.

Berkeley, 1969
Translated by Czesław Miłosz and Lillian Vallee

Temptation

UNDER a starry sky I was taking a walk,
On a ridge overlooking neon cities,
With my companion, the spirit of desolation,
Who was running around and sermonizing,
Saying that I was not necessary, for if not I, then someone else
Would be walking here, trying to understand his age.
Had I died long ago nothing would have changed.
The same stars, cities, and countries
Would have been seen with other eyes.
The world and its labors would go on as they do.

For Christ's sake, get away from me.
You've tormented me enough, I said.
It's not up to me to judge the calling of men.
And my merits, if any, I won't know anyway.

Berkeley, 1975
Translated by Czesław Miłosz and Lillian Vallee

Idea

AFOOT, on horseback, with bugles and baying hounds,
We looked down at last on the wilderness of the Idea,
Sulphur yellow like an aspen forest in late fall
(If the memory of a previous life does not deceive me),
Though it was not a wood, but a tangle of inorganic forms,
Chlorine vapor and mercury and iridescence of crystals.
I glanced at our company: bows, muskets,
A five-shot rifle, here and there a sling.
And the outfits! The latest fashions from the year one thousand
Or, for variety, top hats such as Kierkegaard,
The preacher, used to wear on his walks.
Not an imposing crew. Though, in fact, the Idea
Was dangerous to our kind no more, even in its lair.
To assault poor shepherds, farmhands, lumberjacks
Was its specialty, since it had changed its habits.
And the youngsters above all. Tormenting them with dreams
Of justice on earth and the Island of the Sun.

Berkeley, 1976
Translated by Czesław Miłosz and Robert Hass

A Poetic State

AS IF I were given a reversed telescope instead of eyes, the world moves away and everything grows smaller, people, streets, trees, but they do not lose their distinctness, are condensed.

In the past I had such moments writing poems, so I know distance, disinterested contemplation, putting on an "I" which is not "I," but now it is like that constantly and I ask myself what it means, whether I have entered a permanent poetic state.

Things once difficult are easy, but I feel no strong need to communicate them in writing.

Now I am in good health, where before I was sick because time galloped and I was tortured by fear of what would happen next.

Every minute the spectacle of the world astonishes me; it is so comic that I cannot understand how literature could expect to cope with it.

Sensing every minute, in my flesh, by my touch, I tame misfortune and do not ask God to avert it, for why should He avert it from me if He does not avert it from others?

I dreamt that I found myself on a narrow ledge over the water where large sea fish were moving. I was afraid I would fall if I looked down, so I turned, gripped with my fingers at the roughness of the stone wall, and moving slowly, with my back to the sea, I reached a safe place.

I was impatient and easily irritated by time lost on trifles among which I ranked cleaning and cooking. Now, attentively, I cut onions, squeeze lemons, and prepare various kinds of sauces.

Berkeley, 1977
Translated by Czesław Miłosz and Robert Hass

Distance

AT A CERTAIN distance I follow behind you, ashamed to come closer.
Though you have chosen me as a worker in your vineyard and I pressed
   the grapes of your wrath.
To every one according to his nature: what is crippled should not always
   be healed.
I do not even know whether one can be free, for I have toiled against
   my will.
Taken by the neck like a boy who kicks and bites
Till they sit him at the desk and order him to make letters,
I wanted to be like others but was given the bitterness of separation,
Believed I would be an equal among equals but woke up a stranger.
Looking at manners as if I arrived from a different time.
Guilty of apostasy from the communal rite.
There are so many who are good and just, those were rightly chosen
And wherever you walk the earth, they accompany you.
Perhaps it is true that I loved you secretly
But without strong hope to be close to you as they are.

Berkeley, 1980
Translated by Czesław Miłosz and Robert Hass

Bypassing Rue Descartes

BYPASSING rue Descartes
I descended toward the Seine, shy, a traveler,
A young barbarian just come to the capital of the world.

We were many, from Jassy and Koloshvar, Wilno and Bucharest, Saigon
   and Marrakesh,
Ashamed to remember the customs of our homes,
About which nobody here should ever be told:
The clapping for servants, barefooted girls hurry in,
Dividing food with incantations,
Choral prayers recited by master and household together.

I had left the cloudy provinces behind,
I entered the universal, dazzled and desiring.

Soon enough, many from Jassy and Koloshvar, or Saigon or Marrakesh
Would be killed because they wanted to abolish the customs of their
   homes.

Soon enough, their peers were seizing power
In order to kill in the name of the universal, beautiful ideas.

Meanwhile the city behaved in accordance with its nature,
Rustling with throaty laughter in the dark,
Baking long breads and pouring wine into clay pitchers,
Buying fish, lemons, and garlic at street markets,
Indifferent as it was to honor and shame and greatness and glory,
Because that had been done already and had transformed itself
Into monuments representing nobody knows whom,
Into arias hardly audible and into turns of speech.

Again I lean on the rough granite of the embankment,
As if I had returned from travels through the underworlds
And suddenly saw in the light the reeling wheel of the seasons
Where empires have fallen and those once living are now dead.

There is no capital of the world, neither here nor anywhere else,
And the abolished customs are restored to their small fame
And now I know that the time of human generations is not like the time
   of the earth.

As to my heavy sins, I remember one most vividly:
How, one day, walking on a forest path along a stream,
I pushed a rock down onto a water snake coiled in the grass.

And what I have met with in life was the just punishment
Which reaches, sooner or later, the breaker of a taboo.

Berkeley, 1980
Translated by Renata Gorczynski and Robert Hass

Rivers

UNDER various names, I have praised only you, rivers!
You are milk and honey and love and death and dance.
From a spring in hidden grottoes, seeping from mossy rocks
Where a goddess pours live water from a pitcher,
At clear streams in the meadow, where rills murmur underground,
Your race and my race begin, and amazement, and quick passage.
Naked, I exposed my face to the sun, steering with hardly a dip of the
    paddle—
Oak woods, fields, a pine forest skimming by,
Around every bend the promise of the earth,
Village smoke, sleepy herds, flights of martins over sandy bluffs.
I entered your waters slowly, step-by-step,
And the current in that silence took me by the knees
Until I surrendered and it carried me and I swam
Through the huge reflected sky of a triumphant noon.
I was on your banks at the onset of midsummer night
When the full moon rolls out and lips touch in the rituals of kissing—
I hear in myself, now as then, the lapping of water by the boathouse
And the whisper that calls me in for an embrace and for consolation.

We go down with the bells ringing in all the sunken cities.

Forgotten, we are greeted by the embassies of the dead,

While your endless flowing carries us on and on;

And neither is nor was. The moment only, eternal.

Berkeley, 1980
Translated by Renata Gorczynski and Robert Hass

Preparation

STILL ONE more year of preparation.
Tomorrow at the latest I'll start working on a great book
In which my century will appear as it really was.
The sun will rise over the righteous and the wicked.
Springs and autumns will unerringly return,
In a wet thicket a thrush will build his nest lined with clay
And foxes will learn their foxy natures.

And that will be the subject, with addenda. Thus: armies
Running across frozen plains, shouting a curse
In a many-voiced chorus; the cannon of a tank
Growing immense at the corner of a street; the ride at dusk
Into a camp with watchtowers and barbed wire.

No, it won't happen tomorrow. In five or ten years.
I still think too much about the mothers
And ask what is man born of woman.
He curls himself up and protects his head
While he is kicked by heavy boots; on fire and running,
He burns with bright flame; a bulldozer sweeps him into a clay pit.
Her child. Embracing a teddy bear. Conceived in ecstasy.

I haven't learned yet to speak as I should, calmly.

Translated by Czesław Miłosz and Robert Hass

Theodicy

No, it won't do, my sweet theologians.
Desire will not save the morality of God.
If he created beings able to choose between good and evil,
And they chose, and the world lies in iniquity,
Nevertheless, there is pain, and the undeserved torture of creatures,
Which would find its explanation only by assuming
The existence of an archetypal Paradise
And a pre-human downfall so grave
That the world of matter received its shape from diabolic power.

Translated by Czesław Miłosz and Robert Hass

Poet at Seventy

Thus, brother theologian, here you are,
Connoisseur of heavens and abysses,
Year after year perfecting your art,
Choosing bookish wisdom for your mistress,
Only to discover you wander in the dark.

Ai, humiliated to the bone
By tricks that crafty reason plays,
You searched for peace in human homes
But they, like sailboats, glide away,
Their goal and port, alas, unknown.

You sit in taverns drinking wine,
Pleased by the hubbub and the din,
Voices grow loud and then decline
As if played out by a machine
And you accept your quarantine.

On this sad earth no time to grieve,
Love potions every spring are brewing,
Your heart, in magic, finds relief,
Though Lenten dirges cut your cooing.
And thus you learn how to forgive.

Voracious, frivolous, and dazed
As if your time were without end
You run around and loudly praise
Theatrum where the flesh pretends
To win the game of nights and days.

In plumes and scales to fly and crawl,
Put on mascara, fluffy dresses,
Attempt to play like beast and fowl,
Forgetting interstellar spaces:
Try, my philosopher, this world.

And all your wisdom came to nothing
Though many years you worked and strived
With only one reward and trophy:
Your happiness to be alive
And sorrow that your life is closing.

Translated by Czesław Miłosz

A Confession

MY LORD, I loved strawberry jam
And the dark sweetness of a woman's body.
Also well-chilled vodka, herring in olive oil,
Scents, of cinnamon, of cloves.
So what kind of prophet am I? Why should the spirit
Have visited such a man? Many others
Were justly called, and trustworthy.
Who would have trusted me? For they saw
How I empty glasses, throw myself on food,
And glance greedily at the waitress's neck.
Flawed and aware of it. Desiring greatness,
Able to recognize greatness wherever it is,
And yet not quite, only in part, clairvoyant,
I know what was left for smaller men like me:
A feast of brief hopes, a rally of the proud.
A tournament of hunchbacks, literature.

Berkeley, 1985
Translated by Czesław Miłosz and Robert Hass

How It Should Be in Heaven

HOW IT should be in Heaven I know, for I was there.
By its river. Listening to its birds.
In its season: in summer, shortly after sunrise.
I would get up and run to my thousand works
And the garden was superterrestrial, owned by imagination.
I spent my life composing rhythmical spells
Not quite aware of what was happening to me.
But striving, chasing without cease
A name and a form. I think the movement of blood
Should continue there to be a triumphant one,
Of a higher, I would say, degree. That the smell of gillyflower,
That a nasturtium and a bee and a ladybug
Or their very essence, stronger than here,
Must summon us just the same to a core, to a center
Beyond the labyrinth of things. For how could the mind
Stop its hunt, if from the Infinite
It takes enchantment, avidity, promise?
But where is our, dear to us, mortality?
Where is time that both destroys and save us?
This is too difficult for me. Peace eternal
Could have no mornings and no evenings,
Such a deficiency speaks against it.
And that's too hard a nut for a theologian to crack.

Rome, 1986
Translated by Czesław Miłosz and Robert Hass

Caffé Greco

IN THE eighties of the twentieth century, in Rome, via Condotti
We were sitting with Turowicz in the Caffé Greco
And I spoke in, more or less, these words:

—We have seen much, comprehended much.
States were falling, countries passed away.
Chimeras of the human mind besieged us
And made people perish or sink into slavery.
The swallows of Rome wake me up at dawn
And I feel then transitoriness, the lightness

Of detaching myself. Who I am, who I was
Is not so important. Because others,
Noble-minded, great, sustain me
Anytime I think of them. Of the hierarchy of beings.
Those who gave testimony to their faith,
Whose names are erased or trampled to the ground
Continue to visit us. From them we take the measure,
Aesthetic, I should say, of works, expectations, designs.
By what can literature redeem itself
If not by a melopoeia of praise, a hymn
Even unintended? And you have my admiration,
For you accomplished more than did my companions
Who once sat here, the proud geniuses.
Why they grieved over their lack of virtue,
Why they felt such pangs of conscience, I now understand.
With age and with the waning of this age
One learns to value wisdom, and simple goodness.
Maritain whom we used to read long ago
Would have reason to be glad. And for me: amazement
That the city of Rome stands, that we meet again,
That I still exist for a moment, myself and the swallows.

Rome, 1986
Translated by Czesław Miłosz and Robert Hass

And Yet the Books

AND YET the books will be there on the shelves, separate beings,
That appeared once, still wet
As shining chestnuts under a tree in autumn,
And, touched, coddled, began to live
In spite of fires on the horizon, castles blown up,
Tribes on the march, planets in motion.
"We are," they said, even as their pages
Were being torn out, or a buzzing flame
Licked away their letters. So much more durable
Than we are, whose frail warmth
Cools down with memory, disperses, perishes.
I imagine the earth when I am no more:

Nothing happens, no loss, it's still a strange pageant,
Women's dresses, dewy lilacs, a song in the valley.
Yet the books will be there on the shelves, well born,
Derived from people, but also from radiance, heights.

Berkeley, 1986
Translated by Czesław Miłosz and Robert Hass

1945

—YOU! THE LAST Polish poet!—drunk, he embraced me,
My friend from the Avant-Garde, in a long military coat,
Who had lived through the war in Russia and, there, understood.

He could not have learned those things from Apollinaire,
Or Cubist manifestos, or the festivals of Paris streets.
The best cure for illusions is hunger, patience, and obedience.

In their fine capitals they still liked to talk.
Yet the twentieth century went on. It was not they
Who would decide what words were going to mean.

On the steppe, as he was binding his bleeding feet with a rag
He grasped the futile pride of those lofty generations.
As far as he could see, a flat, unredeemed earth.

Gray silence settled over every tribe and people.
After the bells of baroque churches, after a hand on a saber,
After disputes over free will, and arguments of diets.

I blinked, ridiculous and rebellious,
Alone with my Jesus Mary against irrefutable power,
A descendant of ardent prayers, of gilded sculptures and miracles.

And I knew I would speak in the language of the vanquished
No more durable than old customs, family rituals,
Christmas tinsel, and once a year the hilarity of carols.

Berkeley, 1985
Translated by Czesław Miłosz and Robert Hass

Jan Twardowski
1915–

The World

GOD HID himself so that the world could be seen
if he'd made himself known there would only be him
and who in his presence would notice the ant
the handsome, peevish wasp worrying in circles
the green drake with his yellow legs
the peewit laying its four eggs crosswise
the dragonfly's round eyes beans in the pod
our mother at the table holding not so long ago
a mug by its big funny ear
the fir tree shedding husks instead of cones
pain and delight both ways to learn
equally mysteries but never the same
stones which show travelers the way

love that is invisible
hides nothing

Hungry

MY GOD is hungry
he's just a bag of bones
he's got no money
no lofty silver domes

Candles can't help him
hymns give him no rest
doctors have no cure
for his thin hollow chest

Governments patrols police
are powerless
love is the only food
his lips will bless

The Jesus of Nonbelievers

THE JESUS of nonbelievers
walks among us
known a little from kitsch
and a bit from word-of-mouth
responsibly passed over
in the morning paper
defenseless
partyless
endlessly debated
avoided like a graveyard
for the victims of the plague
necessarily gray
therefore perfectly safe

the Jesus of nonbelievers
walks among us
sometimes he stops
and stands like a hard cross

believers nonbelievers
we'll all be joined
by the unearned pain
that leads us toward truth

As It Must

YOU GRASSHOPPER with only one autumn to live
you unloved loving heart
you sadness just for the two
who'll get their apartment in twenty years
you happiness more or less

you wounding truth
you aunt on whose ID some kid has scrawled a beard
you dignitary soon to be booted downstairs

all will be as it must

Asking for Faith

I'M KNOCKING at heaven
and asking for faith
but not the makeshift kind
that counts the stars but doesn't notice chickens
not the butterfly kind that lasts a day
I want
the kind that's always fresh because it's boundless
that follows its mother like a lamb
that doesn't grasp but understands
that picks the smallest words
can't answer everything
and doesn't come undone
if someone croaks

Witold Wirpsza
1918–85

Mendacity

SENSIBLE, sensitive people are doomed to
Mendacity: opposing truths couple
In them and multiply, and couple again; the
Same thing goes for opposing
Lies, and also, though less frequently,
For truths and lies together, and so
The whirling web knots on, a frenzied dance

Which it would be a shame to stop.

Mendacity, if it's deliberate (and based,
Moreover, on sensitivity and sense), is
Complex, inward work with great
Philosophical merit; the goal is reaching
Harmony: between opposing
Truths and lies, and other
Equally opposing things. Beyond
Mendacity's inward realms, such harmony is
Out of reach, and this, after all, is a classical ballet

Which it would be a shame to stop.

Berlin, June 1974

The Dance of the Asphyxiated
Edel sei der Mensch, hilfreich und gut.
Goethe

NOBLE, helpful, good.
They know it by heart, poor things, and
They don't see that these are the staves of a tripod on which sits
Not a cobbler but a Pythia, and not even
A Pythia but a witch who mumbles and mutters, but knows

Damn well what she means. In front of her, moreover,
A cauldron's hanging on
Another three staves (baseness,
Egoism, evil): a fire burns
Beneath it, a brew churns
Inside it, a stupefying brew.
And they, poor things, look at what's beneath
The witch's bottom and believe
That their inebriation emanates
From the staves of nobility, etc.; oblivious,
They inhale the brew's fumes and
Stagger blindly around
The tripods (noticing only the one),
Convinced that their staggering
Is dance and harmony. Since the landscape
Is rocky, one day they'll smash
Their heads against the stones.
Pythia
        (the witch) will keep on
Muttering after their death, with her
Bottom planted firmly on the staves
Of goodness, etc., knowing
Damn well what she means.

Berlin, July 1974

Footnote

(From the poem "Forecast")

(Hamlet gets off a train; Fortinbras is waiting on the platform)

HAMLET
My Fortinbras, I've just come back
From the other world, where it seems
That my neurotic question—to be
Or not to be—is pretty meaningless.
On stage you can tease the audience;
In the afterlife there's no one left to tease.
Back to the castle, someone's got to govern
Denmark. Today I'd like to take a look
At the bookkeeping and at the pacts you signed

With the Czechs, the French, the Chinese, and the Swedes.
Did you wage any wars? Did you pillage the Turks?
My Fortinbras, I've come back from nothingness
Which differs from being only in that
There is no being in nothingness, whereas in being there is.
But here, in Denmark, while I was away,
The Danes lived on, and no one thought to ask
About being or not. So I've come back to check
On how you've managed since the massacre.

The Law of Asylum

ASILÓN, a place of refuge, an
Escape. But where to hide your harried
Head? Neither the Greeks nor
The Romans knew this
Alliterated "h" although they too at times
Had harried heads and knew
The law of asylum. *Asyle des alliénés:*
And harried, hapless, homeless
Heads are precisely the point.
                              Heads.
But what about the rest of the body? Where
Is the asylum for listless lungs
And stodgy stomachs, hurt hearts,
Lethargic livers, slippery spleens? Are there
Specialized asylums for the separate organs

And what registers do these organs have?
Vox humana? Who pulls the
Registers from their stops and shelves, who
Draws up lists, who keeps files
On these organic registers, this
Organized orgy, this normalized enormity?

There are files and registers; and there
May be asylum. But the law (of asylum
And non-asylum) is just for heads. For
Hammering heads.
                    Head against head,
Head-on, and head over heels, knock

And a head shall be opened,
Hard-hitting alliterative
"H," a law known to the ancients,
Though without alliteration.

Asilón tout court.

Berlin, February 1976

Speech

(From the poem *Liturgy*)

THE WORD will not be addressed; it does not befit a sinner.
   Language, however,
Is too precise. Speech is inexact; therefore I will
Speak of it. The trouble is that one can speak of anything
And anything can be speech; even the unspeakable.

The trickiest shadow, cast by fly or bird
On stone or water speaks if it is seen; the simplest
Gesture speaks if I make it in a cave; a child's
Lightest dance will speak if his lungs hold music; the greatest
Weight, if it falls, resounds in the abyss.

The same may be said of tears and open grief,
Of an unsightly face, if one elaborates, of
Up and down staircases, a woodborer's tapping, a tire's screech.
A conductor sets off eloquent changes
In harmony's shifting system with a flick
Of his eyelid alone, though his music stand is
Empty and his hand remains unseen.

Spots on human skin, a ship's rotating blade,
Scissors lying crosswise on a desk, mirrors shimmering
In Leonardo's unbuilt labyrinth, a dying woman's aged
Trembling lips: all this proclaims that
All is in its place, the place of speech and lamentation,
Of joy and fear and grief, and freedom and constraint,
And that all this is one place, the place of prayer.

Anna Kamieńska

1920–86

History

WE NO LONGER have history
all we have are wasted
moments of life
forty-eight hours
of mock justice
this is not history these are not its bells
a day's quicksand sinking voices
our funerals in whispering leaves
the embrace above the coffin eyes eyes
and time rolling over us
will not have the face of history
but a fox's sly and treacherous snout

Youth

HE BEATS his head on the table he screams
Where is the record
of everything never recorded
where is the wasted life
the youth snapped in half
the tragedy that's not tragic but
has taken root in our veins
all that we carry within us
that we keep hushed up
that we communicate
by bumping elbows on the street
that we communicate through our breath
on a crowded bus
Where is the witness
where is memory
why do we hand down defeat to defeat

He screams in an ever-louder whisper
So we only read silent novels
of wrinkles weariness wordlessness
death despair
And he wrings his hands choking
on youth's bread of denial

Closed Eyes

THE LITTLE universe you can't escape
the prison cell of our death
earth's leprous skin
the swan's wing stuck in a sea of grease
who remembers the sight of a real sunset
the smell of soil split for seeds
and no gate opens into empty space
except perhaps the one behind closed eyes

Funny

WHAT'S IT like to be a human
the bird asked

I myself don't know
it's being held prisoner by your skin
while reaching infinity
being a captive of your scrap of time
while touching eternity
being hopelessly uncertain
and helplessly hopeful
being a needle of frost
and a handful of heat
breathing in the air
and choking wordlessly
it's being on fire
with a nest made of ashes
eating bread
while filling up on hunger

it's dying without love
it's loving through death

That's funny said the bird
and flew effortlessly up into the air

The Other World

I DON'T believe in the other world

But I don't believe in this one either
unless it's pierced by light

I believe in a woman's body
hit by a car in the street

I believe in bodies
stopped short in mid-rush
mid-gesture mid-push
as if what they'd been waiting for so long
were just about to begin
as if at any minute
a meaning would lift
its index finger up

I believe in the blind eye
the deaf ear
the crippled leg
the crow's foot
the cheek's red flame

I believe in bodies lying
in sleep's deep trust
I believe in age's patience
in unborn frailty

I believe in the one hair that a dead man
left on his brown beret

I believe in a brightness
miraculously increased
to shine on all things

Even on the beetle
that lies wriggling on its back
helpless as a pup

I believe that rain
stitches heaven and earth together
and that angels descend
in this rain visibly
like winged frogs

I don't believe in this world
empty
as a railroad station at dawn
when all the trains have left
for the beyond

The world is one
especially when it wakens in the dew
and the Lord takes a stroll
among the foliage
of human and animal dreams

Two Faiths

To Father Jacek Salij

HE BELIEVES if he believes
in God that He is
vast and indifferent

tangled up in stars
as in the burning bush
a luminous still spider
who hangs above the world

A giant Hebrew letter
with shattered shins
a nocturnal bird of prey
dragging bloodied life
in its beak

He would not dwell
in water churning with spawning fish
in bodies' rotten heat
in the rapt attention of hearts

Bloody history
a child's death
cannot call Him
from Himself

While we eternal prisoners of Auschwitz
think that he went insane with pity
and became one of us
so that he could look into our eyes
with a human face
from a piece of bread

A Cross

IN A DREAM I saw a cross
one arm was short
and the other infinitely long
Some say
it's simple
All problems have already been solved
the burden is light and every tear
will be wiped away
it's enough
to live your life from start to finish
then simply awaken to eternity

But I keep carrying the other arm
the endless one
and I know that the light thing is a burden
that what must be wiped away is a tear
larger than the planet
there are days that drag on longer
than forever
And I can't imagine a death
that means awakening
a darkness

that is light
a moment
that is immortality
a love
that is not you

A Prayer That Will Be Answered

LORD let me suffer much
and then die

Let me walk through silence
and leave nothing behind not even fear

Make the world continue
let the ocean kiss the sand just as before

Let the grass stay green
so that the frogs can hide in it

so that someone can bury his face in it
and sob out his love

Make the day rise brightly
as if there were no more pain

And let my poem stand clear as a windowpane
bumped by a bumblebee's head

Service

WHEN the angel of death entered
he found scattered underwear
a stiffened garter belt
and hands one of which
was reaching for something on the floor
a broken glass
a ballpoint pen under the table

The angel bent and humbly
picked up a crumpled stocking
mindful that death is also service

Julia Hartwig
1921–

In Your Eyes

IN YOUR EYES, Europe, we are history's reservation
with our dated ideals
with our dusted-off treasure box
with the songs we sing
We give up our best
for the dragon of force and violence to devour
The young boys the beautiful girls
the best minds the most auspicious talents
the tribute of flowers crosses words
We the reckless heirs of earnestness
the unordained heralds of hope
inheritors of a native rhetoric
which fits us like a glove
even though yesterday
it still seemed rather tight

But Of Course

BUT OF course you too would make a good martyr
with that poor health of yours with your shortness of breath
with your fussy habits
and your liking for a hot bath every day
But of course No one said anywhere
that you'll always keep on walking deep in thought
with that gentle smile of yours
that one day they won't throw your books about
that blood won't trickle from your beaten face

Above Us

BOYS KICKING a ball on a vast square beneath an obelisk
and the apocalyptic sky at sunset to the rear
Why the sudden menace in this view
as if someone wished to turn it all to red dust
The sun already knows And the sky knows it too
And the water in the river knows
Music bursts from the loudspeakers like wild laughter
Only a star high above us
stands lost in thought with a finger to its lips

What Can They

WHAT CAN the interrogator and the interrogated tell each other?
What is the common language they could speak?
That language is mountains away and there is no fool
who would set out to look for it
The knife enters the animal's flesh without consent or prior inquiries
the apple won't strike up a chat with the rifle bullet cast off in the grass
the liar's tongue turns round like a rotten mill wheel
and the water won't sing in chorus with its creak
Longing for freedom is like a lark flying straight up
toward the face of God and the sun
with unshakable faith that the face will finally be seen
The little lark flies faster than the stone thrown by a foolish bully
Oh the dialogue of the shoe and the crushed weed
the dialogue of the pale warden and the young face paler still
the dialogue of force and martyrdom
cruelty and pain
the martyr and the torturer
before it's cut short
by whom by what when

Toward the End

TOWARD the end you don't really care if you're still yourself
everything that has lived in you has the right to exist
you speak with others' voices
you dream other people's dreams
they can feed you with porridge or tears
no one owes you anything anymore
and you've earned a little of it all
your sins are countless and your love for life spills over
you're a man of the world
but your curiosity isn't yet gone
you take in the twilight on the river till it hurts
you take in the gray engraving of the city in the rain
and the suddenly uncovered sky
cherished by a wreath of clouds
you've never felt such comfort
even though you've never gotten anything said to the end
and all the things you've done are far from perfect
the only art you're learning
is the art of saying good-bye
yet why are you supposed to leave without regret
regret is the only form of payment for what you have received

Before Dawn

WHO DO they work so hard for
what do they call to so stubbornly
repeating the same tune time and again
the same humble motif
sung with royal verve
What in this asphalt suburb
could give them such joy
such ecstasy of prayer while it's still dark
with not a single bright streak in the sky
to announce the dawn's arrival
Ah they know that somewhere far away
but not so far away
that they can't feel it
there are spreading elms

and a grove of airy green full of motion
and brotherly twitters
they know there are gardens standing on tiptoe
on the lookout for the spring's procession
They sense the hurried breath of lilacs
and, beneath the windows, the hyacinths' childish cries
O joyful, cooing birds
why did you wake me in the midst of hope
only to make me listen with despair
I don't know how to respond to your song
I can only strain my ears while I lie still in the dark

Who Says

WHILE THE innocents were being massacred who says
that flowers didn't bloom, that the air didn't breathe bewildering scents
that birds didn't rise to the heights of their most accomplished songs
that young lovers didn't twine in love's embraces
But would it have been fitting if a scribe of the time had shown this
and not the monstrous uproar on a street drenched with blood
the wild screams of mothers with infants torn from their arms
the scuffling, the senseless laughter of soldiers
aroused by the touch of women's bodies and young breasts warm
    with milk
Flaming torches tumbled down stone steps
there seemed no hope of rescue
and violent horror soon gave way to the still more awful
numbness of despair
At that moment covered by the southern night's light shadow
a bearded man leaning on a staff
and a girl with a child in her arms
were fleeing lands ruled by the cruel tyrant
carrying the world's hope to a safer place
beneath silent stars in which these events
had been recorded centuries ago

Your Nature

YOUR NATURE is evil Resign yourself to this
It calls through you with a voice that frightens you
With words you didn't think you had in you
It spurts from you differently than you expected
a boiling spring that smells of sulphur
from which green meadows of seeming grow faint

Hesitating over a Young Poet's Book
(From the sequence "Americana")

THE HOTEL maid will be surprised tomorrow morning
when she finds this book beside the bed
I think I'll leave it here
since my suitcase is already overflowing
Still I compare its weight once more
to the weight of the poems that it holds
His efforts after all are genuine
if in spite of this June heat
I did believe in the November sleet
that drove him to a bar after he had lost his girl
and I believed in that morning when it first dawned on him
how little his family home still meant
so he packed his bags and left forever
He took odd jobs
lived in a hurry woke up in the depths of despair
wishing he could fall asleep and never get up
and he clearly didn't steal these facts from any other life
or these poems from any other book
Doesn't that make his work worth keeping?
I've never been good at getting rid of things anyhow
Everything I come upon I carry in me
like a deposit left waiting by its tardy owner
Maybe they're right
those people who shake off useless things so easily
and head straight for their chosen goal
They must find my wavering laughable

A Need

I BELIEVE in the sentence In the stop which seeks a form
as deft and modest as common speech
Everything within me longs for the moment when a shape
surmounts the shapelessness in which I dangle
and endure the quiet constant pain of indetermination
the dissolving thoughts and feelings
that create my rarefied space
This doesn't keep me from admiring the linden that stretches
branches wide across my window from hearing shrieks
of magpies both a nuisance and a blessing because they exist
it doesn't keep me from taking in the heat
of this dry and tragic summer
But a sentence a solid sentence
restores the earth beneath my feet

Tadeusz Różewicz
1921–

Laughter

THE CAGE stayed shut so long
that a bird was hatched inside

the bird stayed still so long
that the cage
corroded by its silence
opened up

the silence lasted so long
that behind the black bars
laughter rang

Pouring

THIS rustle

it's life pouring
from the world filled with objects
into death

it's through me
a hole
in reality
that this world squeezes its way
into the other world

I think this through
the one whom
I sought above
waits below

in the den
a transfiguration

sluggish mooing
of trumpets made of
kneaded waste paper
and rolled
magazines

a rising from the dead
absentminded
futile

*   *   *

THE POET grows weaker
images lose strength

paints pale fade
melt away
they turn white at the river's mouth
and wash into
a black hole

on October 20, 1850
Arthur Rimbaud
came into the world

Season in Hell
what a glorious age
hell heaven

the metaphor still living
bloomed within
metaphysics

letters and words
appeared in miraculous color
A noir E blanc I rouge
O bleu U vert

Poetry began from that moment
to rave deliriously

between the two wars
images turned white
metaphors turned white

A blanc E blanc I blanc
O blanc U blanc

in the nuclear flash
eyes lips turned white
the world's shape turned white

Artur Międzyrzecki
1922–

At the Cave

YOU CAN come to terms with anyone
Even a troglodyte
You only have to keep your head
To be patient
To offer him a lamb a herd of oxen a few sheep
To figure out his reasons right after he yells
To guess them from his gestures and his glance
When his eyes get bloodshot, then he's mad
Call the soldiers and make them take back what they brought
When he thumps his chest, then he's happy
Order the same thing once again
He drinks sugar water
Alcohol apparently isn't recommended

You have to understand him that's all
Don't meddle with his tastes
Demand the impossible
He's cruel by our standards
But he's got his own logic
This is a different configuration from a different culture
We must make him feel that we can respect it
Show sympathy and kindness
Not provoke him

Fate the Clerk Lays Down a New Set of Bylaws

FATE THE clerk lays down a new set of bylaws
It used to be the elements' decree now it's a decree of the authorities
Hard to believe that back then it was personal like a soul
On a first-name basis with those wretched kings in their nooses

It's gotten red-tapey and torpid
It's a bookkeeper of great numbers
It still cuts down a forest or a nation the way it did before
But now it's hit-or-miss and get-out-if-you-can

29-77-02

REALISTIC dreams with a whiff of terror
I've got to call the number 29 77 02
I call with no luck from God knows what cities
I want to talk to the beautiful M. S.
We were friends ages ago
But she's either dead or forgotten
The phone booths are dusty and dark
The dials are falling off or don't work
We're sitting with Julia at a table covered in white
It's a party thrown by our classmates' parents
We don't know anyone there
We feel depressed and sad and I wake up
It's the night from March seventh to the eighth in Normandy
I turn on the lamp I write down the phone number
Tugboats call out to each other in the fog

They

DON'T THINK it's your character they don't like
Your weakness, your terrific disposition
Don't think that they don't like your critical mind
Or your unwavering faith
Or the sky-high flight of your unruly soul
Or that you're a slave to love

It's time you knew that they don't like all of you
They don't like you as you are nor anything you say or do
And it's not my place to tell you
What a black and venomous hatred this is
And who the killers of God are
And the destroyers of peoples

The War of Nerves

THE WAR of nerves is a natural phenomenon
Dogs wage it with cats, bears with bees
The pine moth with the forester, the bookworm with the bookseller
The skunk and the boa with the rabbit

Gentle persuasion won't help much here
There's no point dreaming about taking some time off
Since what kind of break will the mountain eagle get
When he's being shot at from a copter

But the nightingale still sings in spite of danger
The soaring eagle holds sway in the spring sky
The swallow flits by, the swift flutters its wings
The woodpecker, gaudy drummer, won't give up its morning scores

In the war of nerves the less-nervous one wins
The one who doesn't borrow trouble and understands
That the skunk won't shake off its skunky nature
And that you've got to keep your inner balance

1981

What Does the Political Scientist Know

WHAT DOES the political scientist know?
The political scientist knows the latest trends
The current states of affairs
The history of doctrines

What does the political scientist not know?
The political scientist doesn't know about desperation
He doesn't know the game that consists
In renouncing the game

It doesn't occur to him
That no one knows when
Irrevocable changes may appear
Like an ice floe's sudden cracks

And that our natural resources
Include knowledge of venerated laws
The capacity for wonder
And a sense of humor

1981

Can You Imagine

ABSENCE
Can you imagine
Absence
Not as the opposite
Of something that is and breathes
Or a gap in the universal presence of things
Or a catchword that calls for a mediating symbol
Or for dialectic quibbles
But as infinite transparence
Where no images take root
A colorless invisible monochrome
Absence
Something that's not there
That's not there anywhere

Let It Talk

LET THE TREE talk which has grown tall within you
Lend a patient ear to the lament of its leaves
Let the birds talk among its boughs

The Reason of Existence

THE ETERNAL quarrel
between the reason of existence and the reason of brute force
reaches exceptional intensity
whenever individual or collective self-conceit

leads to the catastrophe of war
or when tyranny wields its arbitrary power
transgressing humanity's true nature
and the law that sanctifies it

In such cases it's clear
that the reason of brute force—however it's explained—
is always a corruption of life
in its very social essence
which is the endless play
between acquired culture and one's sense of personal uniqueness
between free impulse and an unimagined obligation
to oneself and others

In examining injustices and wrongs
no one can possibly say
if the human reason for existence
must always give way to violence
at least for some period of time

But that's the way it is
and it's not just the result of this or that set
of shifting circumstances
it comes from the black breath of the contrary spirit
from evil hovering

The Golden Age

SO WHAT if clowns and gnomes
Run the show at the royal court
Calabacillas, called the idiot from Coria
Barberousse the coxcomb
Pablo de Valladolid the nitwit reciter

The Golden Age is the Golden Age
Philip the Fourth's favorites have nothing to do with it
Only the scribblers from outside the palace walls count
Góngora Calderón Lope de Vega Tirso de Molina

And who cares after all whom Velázquez paints so beautifully
The grand duke on horseback or the jester Hodson with his dog

1979

Simultaneism

BUT THIS is happening
Simultaneously!
Simultaneously!
So what
If it's happening simultaneously?
Could anyone at any time
Have had the slightest doubt
That everything always and everywhere
Happens simultaneously?
Air raid sirens and drifting clouds
And the grip of the invisible paw
That suddenly grasps your throat
And you feel the air and blood that circulate
Within you shutting off
While for some unknown reason
A buzzing meadow from the past comes back to you
And you hear robins and larks sing
And the Falklands war begins
And they play taps in Kraków and a passenger plane
Takes off from the Long Island airport
And you love and lose and you repeat
The coded gestures of despair
And deeply hurt and hurting
You burst like shrapnel
In all parts of your deep heaven
And you don't know about the hundred things
Happening at this very moment
Simultaneously!
Simultaneously!
Oh don't even try to reassemble them
In your multilayered narratives:
The descriptive disease is no better than the rest
And includes confusion of measures
A Saint Vitus dance of glances
Obfuscation of speech

Someone Else

A TYRANT'S proclamations (in whatever era)
Are merely words

Someone else must translate them into a manhunt
Someone with a knack
Someone who likes his work

Someone adept at getting the right people
To the right place at the right time
To pound on the door with a crowbar or a fist

Someone who draws up the timetables for raids
As if they were crosswords in the Sunday paper

Someone who doesn't bother with whatever's coming next
It's no longer his affair
He's not responsible
Hell's humble servant
An exemplary employee an adroit technician

Obituary

HE KNEW how to barter
But he couldn't sell himself

He knew how to have his say
But he listened with just one ear

He could go to great lengths
But he couldn't get back

His love was larger than life
But his life was very small

Wisława Szymborska
1923–

Stage Fright

POETS AND writers.
So the saying goes.
That is poets aren't writers, but who—

Poets are poetry, writers are prose—

Prose can hold anything including poetry
but in poetry there's only room for poetry—

In keeping with the poster that announces it
with a fin-de-siècle flourish of its giant P
framed in a winged lyre's strings
I shouldn't simply walk in, I should fly—

And wouldn't I be better-off barefoot
to escape the clump and squeak
of cut-rate sneakers,
a clumsy ersatz angel—

If at least the dress were longer and more flowing
and the poems appeared not from a handbag but by sleight-of-hand,
dressed in their Sunday best from head to toe,
with bells on, ding to dong,
ab ab ba—

On the platform lurks a little table
suggesting seances, with gilded legs,
and on the little table smokes a little candlestick—

Which means
I've got to read by candlelight
what I wrote by the light of an ordinary bulb
to the typewriter's tap tap tap—

Without worrying in advance
if it was poetry
and if so, what kind—

The kind in which prose is inappropriate
or the kind which is apropos in prose—

And what's the difference,
seen now only in half-light
against a crimson curtain's
purple fringe?

Surplus

A NEW STAR has been discovered,
which doesn't mean that things have gotten brighter
or that something we've been missing has appeared.

The star is large and distant,
so distant that it's small,
even smaller than others
much smaller than it.
Small wonder, then, if we were struck with wonder;
as we would be if only we had the time.

The star's age, mass, location—
all this perhaps will do
for one doctoral dissertation
and a wine-and-cheese reception
in circles close to the sky:
the astronomer, his wife, friends, and relations,
casual, congenial, come as you are
mostly chat on earthbound topics,
surrounded by cozy earth tones.

The star's superb,
but that's no reason
why we can't drink to the ladies
who are incalculably closer.

The star's inconsequential.
It has no impact on the weather, fashion, final score,
government shake-ups, moral crises, take-home pay.

No effect on propaganda or on heavy industry.
It's not reflected in a conference table's shine.
It's supernumerary in the light of life's numbered days.

What's the use of asking
under how many stars man is born
and under how many in a moment he will die.

A new one.
"At least show me where it is."
"Between that gray cloud's jagged edge
and the acacia twig over there on the left."
"I see," I say.

Archaeology

WELL, MY poor man,
seems we've made some progress in my field.
Millennia have passed
since you first called me archaeology.

I no longer require
your stone gods,
your ruins with legible inscriptions.

Show me your whatever
and I'll tell you who you were.
Something's bottom,
something's top.
A scrap of engine. A picture tube's neck.
An inch of cable. Fingers turned to dust.
Or even less than that, or even less.

Using a method
that you couldn't have known then
I can stir up memory
in countless elements.
Traces of blood are forever.
Lies shine.
Secret codes resound.
Doubts and intentions come to light.

If I want to
(and you can't be too sure
that I will),
I'll peer down the throat of your silence,

I'll read your views
from the sockets of your eyes,
I'll remind you in infinite detail
of what you expected from life besides death.

Show me your nothing
that you've left behind
and I'll build from it a forest and a highway,
an airport, baseness, tenderness,
a missing home.

Show me your little poem
and I'll tell you why it wasn't written
any earlier or later than it was.

On no, you've got me wrong.
Keep your funny piece of paper
with its scribbles.
All I need for my ends
is your layer of dirt
and the long gone
smell of burning.

View with a Grain of Sand

WE CALL IT a grain of sand
but it calls itself neither grain nor sand.
It does just fine without a name,
whether general, particular,
permanent, passing,
incorrect or apt.

Our glance, our touch mean nothing to it.
It doesn't feel itself seen and touched.
And that it fell on the windowsill
is only our experience, not its.
For it it's no different than falling on anything else
with no assurance that it's finished falling
or that it's falling still.

The window has a wonderful view of a lake
but the view doesn't view itself.

It exists in this world
colorless, shapeless,
soundless, odorless, and painless.

The lake's floor exists floorlessly
and its shore exists shorelessly.
Its water feels itself neither wet nor dry
and its waves to themselves are neither singular nor plural.
They splash deaf to their own noise
on pebbles neither large nor small.

And all this beneath a sky by nature skyless
in which the sun sets without setting at all
and hides without hiding behind an unminding cloud.
The wind ruffles it, its only reason being
that it blows.

A second passes.
A second second.
A third.
But they're three seconds only for us.

Time has passed like a courier with urgent news.
But that's just our simile.
The character's invented, his haste is make-believe,
his news inhuman.

Clothes

YOU TAKE off, we take off, they take off
coats, jackets, blouses, double-breasted suits
made of wool, cotton, cotton-polyester,
skirts, shirts, underwear, slacks, slips, socks,
putting, hanging, tossing them across
the backs of chairs, the wings of metal screens;
for now, the doctor says, it's not too bad,
you may get dressed, get rested up, get out of town,
take one in case, at bedtime, after lunch,
show up in a couple months, next spring, next year;
you see, and you thought, and we were afraid that,
and he imagined, and you all believed;
it's time to tie, to fasten with shaking hands

shoelaces, buckles, Velcro, zippers, snaps,
belts, buttons, cufflinks, collars, neckties, clasps
and to pull out of handbags, pockets, sleeves
a crumpled, dotted, flowered, chequered scarf
whose usefulness has been suddenly prolonged.

On Death, without Exaggeration

IT CAN'T take a joke,
find a star, make a bridge,
it knows nothing about weaving, mining, farming,
building ships or baking cakes.

In our planning for tomorrow
it has the final word
which is always beside the point.

It can't even get the things done
that are part of its trade:
dig a grave,
make a coffin,
clean up after itself.

Preoccupied with killing,
it does the job awkwardly,
without system or skill.
As though each of us were its first kill.

Oh, it has its triumphs,
but look at its countless defeats,
missed blows
and repeat attempts!

Sometimes it isn't strong enough
to swat a fly from the air.
Many's the caterpillar
that has out-crawled it.

All those bulbs, pods,
tentacles, fins, tracheae,
nuptial plumage and winter fur
show that it's fallen behind
with its half-hearted work.

Ill will won't help
and even our lending a hand with wars and coups d'état
is so far not enough.

Hearts beat inside eggs.
Babies' skeletons grow.
Seeds, hard at work, sprout their first tiny pair of leaves
and sometimes even tall trees far away.

Whoever claims that it's omnipotent,
is himself living proof
that it's not.

There's no life
that couldn't be immortal
if only for a moment.

Death
always arrives by that very moment too late.

In vain it tugs at the knob
of the invisible door.
As far as you've come
can't be undone.

The Great Man's House

THE MARBLE tells us in golden syllables:
Here the great man lived, and worked, and died.
Here are the garden paths where he personally scattered the gravel.
Here's the bench—don't touch—he hewed the stone himself.
And here—watch the steps—we enter the house.

He managed to come into the world at what was still a fitting time.
All that was to pass passed in this house.
Not in housing projects,
not in furnished but empty quarters,
among unknown neighbors,
on fifteenth floors
that student field trips rarely reach.

In this room he thought,
in this alcove he slept,

and here he entertained his guests.
Portraits, armchair, desk, pipe, globe,
flute, well-worn carpet, glassed-in porch.
Here he exchanged bows with the tailor and shoemaker
who made his coats and boots to order.

It's not the same as photographs in boxes,
dried-out ballpoint pens in plastic cups,
store-bought clothes in store-bought closets,
a window that looks out on clouds, not passersby.

Was he happy? Sad?
That's not the point.
He still made confessions in letters
without thinking they'd be opened en route.
He still kept a careful, candid diary
knowing it wouldn't be seized in a search.
The thing that most frightened him was a comet's flight.
The world's doom lay then in God's hands alone.

He was lucky enough to die not in a hospital,
not behind some white, anonymous screen.
There was still someone there at his bedside to memorize
his mumbled words.

As if he had been given
a reusable life:
he sent out books to be bound,
he didn't strike the names of the dead from his ledgers.
And the trees that he planted in the garden by his house
still grew for him as *Juglans regia*
and *Quercus rubra*, and *Ulmus*, and *Larix*,
and *Fraxinus excelsior*.

In Broad Daylight

HE WOULD
vacation in a mountain boardinghouse, he would
come down for lunch, from his
table by the window he would
scan the four spruces, branch to branch,
without shaking off the freshly fallen snow.

Goateed, balding,
gray-haired, in glasses,
with coarsened, weary features,
with a wart on his cheek and a furrowed forehead,
as if clay had covered up the angelic marble—he wouldn't
know himself when it all happened.
The price, after all, for not having died already
goes up not in leaps but step-by-step, and he would
pay that price, too.
About his ear, just grazed by the bullet
when he ducked at the last minute, he would
say: "I was damn lucky."

While waiting to be served his noodle soup, he would
read a paper with the current date,
giant headlines, tiny print of ads,
or drum his fingers on the white tablecloth, and his hands would
have been used a long time now,
with their chapped skin and swollen veins.

Sometimes someone would
yell from the doorway: "Mr. Baczyński, phone call for you"—
and there'd be nothing strange about that
being him, about him standing up, straightening his sweater,
and slowly moving toward the door.

At this sight no one would
stop talking, no one would
freeze in mid-gesture, mid-breath
because this commonplace event would
be treated—such a pity—
as a commonplace event.

Our Ancestors' Short Lives

FEW OF them made it to thirty.
Old age was the privilege of rocks and trees.
Childhood ended as fast as wolf cubs grow.
One had to hurry, to get on with life
before the sun went down,
before the first snow.

Thirteen-year-olds bearing children,
four-year-olds stalking birds' nests in the rushes,
leading the hunt at twenty—
they aren't yet, then they are gone.
Infinity's ends fused quickly.
Witches chewed charms
with all the teeth of youth intact.
A son grew to manhood beneath his father's eye.
Beneath the grandfather's blank sockets the grandson was born.

And anyway they didn't count the years.
They counted nets, pots, sheds, and axes.
Time, so generous toward any petty star in the sky,
offered them a nearly empty hand
and quickly took it back, as if the effort were too much.
One step more, two steps more
along the glittering river
which sprang from darkness and vanished into darkness.

There wasn't a moment to lose,
no deferred questions, no belated revelations,
just those experienced in time.
Wisdom couldn't wait for gray hair.
It had to see clearly before it saw the light
and to hear every voice before it sounded.

Good and evil—
they knew little of them, but knew all:
when evil triumphs, good goes into hiding;
when good is manifest, then evil lies low.
Neither can be conquered
or cast off beyond return.
Hence, if joy, then with a touch of fear,
if despair, then not without some quiet hope.
Life, however long, will always be short.
Too short for anything to be added.

Hitler's First Photograph

AND WHO'S this little fellow in his itty-bitty robe?
That's tiny baby Adolf, the Hitlers' little boy!
Will he grow up to be an LL.D.?
Or a tenor in Vienna's Opera House?
Whose teensy hand is this, whose little ear and eye and nose?
Whose tummy full of milk, we just don't know:
printer's, doctor's, merchant's, priest's?
Where will those tootsy-wootsies finally wander?
To a garden, to a school, to an office, to a bride,
maybe to the Burgermeister's daughter?

Precious little angel, mommy's sunshine, honeybun,
while he was being born a year ago,
there was no dearth of signs on the earth and in the sky:
spring sun, geraniums in windows,
the organ-grinder's music in the yard,
a lucky fortune wrapped in rosy paper,
then just before the labor his mother's fateful dream:
a dove seen in a dream means joyful news,
if it is caught, a long-awaited guest will come.
Knock knock, who's there, it's Adolf's heartchen knocking.

A little pacifier, diaper, rattle, bib,
our bouncing boy, thank God and knock on wood, is well,
looks just like his folks, like a kitten in a basket,
like the tots in every other family album.
Shush, let's not start crying, sugar,
the camera will click from under that black hood.

The Klinger Atelier, Grabenstrasse, Braunau,
and Braunau is a small but worthy town,
honest businesses, obliging neighbors,
smell of yeast dough, of gray soap.
No one hears howling dogs, or fate's footsteps.
A history teacher loosens his collar
and yawns over homework.

The Century's Decline

OUR 20TH century was going to improve on the others.
It will never prove it now,
now that its years are numbered,
its gait is shaky,
its breath is short.

Too many things have happened
that weren't supposed to happen,
and what was supposed to come about,
has not.

Happiness and spring, among other things,
were supposed to be getting closer.

Fear was expected to leave the mountains and the valleys.
Truth was supposed to hit home
before a lie.

A couple of problems weren't going
to come up any more,
hunger, for example,
and war, and so forth.

There was going to be respect
for helpless people's helplessness,
trust, that kind of stuff.

Anyone who planned to enjoy the world
is now faced
with a hopeless task.

Stupidity isn't funny.
Wisdom isn't gay.
Hope
isn't that young girl anymore,
etcetera, alas.

God was finally going to believe
in a man both good and strong,
but good and strong
are still two different men.

"How should we live?" someone asked me in a letter.
I had meant to ask him
the same question.

Again, and as ever,
as may be seen above,
the most pressing questions
are naive ones.

Children of Our Age

WE ARE children of our age,
it's a political age.

All day long, all through the night
all affairs—yours, ours, theirs—
are political affairs.

Whether you like it or not,
your genes have a political past,
your skin—a political cast,
your eyes—a political slant.

Whatever you say reverberates,
whatever you don't say speaks for itself—
so either way you're talking politics.

Even when you take to the woods,
you're taking political steps
on political grounds.

Apolitical poems are also political,
and above us shines a moon
no longer purely lunar.
To be or not to be, that is the question.
And though it troubles the digestion,
it's a question, as always, of politics.

To acquire a political meaning
you don't even have to be human.
Raw material will do,
or protein feed, or crude oil,

or a conference table, whose shape
was quarreled over for months:
should we arbitrate life and death
at a round table or a square one.

Meanwhile people perished,
animals died,
houses burned,
and the fields ran wild
just as in times immemorial
and less political.

Tortures

NOTHING has changed.
The body is a reservoir of pain,
it has to eat and breathe the air, and sleep,
it's got thin skin and the blood is just beneath it,
it's got a good supply of teeth and fingernails,
its bones can be broken, its joints can be stretched.
In tortures, all of this is considered.

Nothing has changed.
The body still trembles as it trembled
before Rome was founded and after,
in the twentieth century before and after Christ;
tortures are just what they were, only the earth has shrunk
and whatever goes on sounds as if it's just a room away.

Nothing has changed.
Except there are more people,
and new offenses have sprung up beside the old ones,
real, make-believe, short-lived, and nonexistent,
but the cry with which the body answers for them
was, is, and will be a cry of innocence
in keeping with the age-old scale and pitch.

Nothing has changed.
Except perhaps the manners, ceremonies, dances.
The gesture of the hands shielding the head
has nonetheless remained the same.
The body writhes, jerks, and tugs,
falls to the ground when shoved, pulls up its knees,
bruises, swells, drools, and bleeds.

Nothing has changed.
Except the run of rivers,
the shapes of forests, shores, deserts, and glaciers.
The little soul roams among those landscapes,
disappears, returns, draws near, moves away,
evasive and a stranger to itself,
now sure, now uncertain of its own existence,
whereas the body is and is and is
and has nowhere to go.

Plotting with the Dead

UNDER WHAT conditions do you dream of the dead?
Do you often think of them before you fall asleep?
Who appears first?
Is it always the same one?
First name? Surname? Cemetery? Date deceased?

To what do they refer?
Old friendship? Kinship? Fatherland?
Do they say where they come from?
And who's behind them?
And who besides you sees them in his dreams?

Their faces, are they like their photographs?
Have they aged at all with time?
Are they robust? Are they wan?
The murdered ones, have their wounds healed yet?
Do they still remember who killed them?

What do they hold in their hands? Describe these objects.
Are they charred? Moldy? Rusty? Decomposed?
And in their eyes, what? Entreaty? A threat? Be specific.
Do you only chat about the weather?
Or about flowers? Birds? Butterflies?

No awkward questions on their part?
If so, what do you reply?
Instead of safely keeping quiet?
Or evasively changing the dream's subject?
Or waking up just in time?

Writing a Résumé

WHAT NEEDS to be done?
Fill out the application
and enclose a résumé.

Regardless of the length of life
a résumé is best kept short.

Concise, well-chosen facts are de rigueur.
Landscapes are replaced by addresses,
shaky memories give way to unshakable dates.

Of all your loves mention only the marriage,
of all your children only those who were born.

Who knows you counts more than who you know.
Trips only if taken abroad.
Memberships in what but without why.
Honors, but not how they were earned.

Write as if you'd never talked to yourself
and always kept yourself at arm's length.

Pass over in silence your dogs, cats, birds,
dusty keepsakes, friends, and dreams.

Price, not worth,
and title, not what's inside.
His shoe size, not where he's off to,
that one you pass yourself off as.

In addition, a photograph with one ear showing.
What matters is its shape, not what it hears.
What is there to hear, anyway?
The clatter of paper shredders.

Funeral

"SO SUDDENLY, who could have seen it coming"
"stress and smoking, I kept telling him"
"not bad, thanks, and you"
"these flowers need to be unwrapped"
"his brother's heart gave out too, it runs in the family"
"I'd never know you in that beard"
"he was asking for it, always mixed up in something"
"that new guy was going to make a speech, I don't see him"
"Kazek's in Warsaw, Tadek's gone abroad"
"you were smart, you brought the only umbrella"
"so what if he was more talented than them"
"no, it's a walk-through room, Barbara won't take it"
"of course he was right, but that's no excuse"
"with bodywork and paint, just guess how much"
"two egg yolks and a tablespoon of sugar"
"none of his business, what was in it for him"
"only in blue and just small sizes"
"five times and never any answer"
"all right, so I could have, but you could have too"
"good thing that at least she still has a job"
"don't know, relatives, I guess"
"that priest looks just like Belmondo"
"I've never been in this part of the grounds"
"I dreamed about him last week, I had a feeling"
"his daughter's not bad looking"
"the way of all flesh"
"give my best to the widow, I've got to run"
"it all sounded so much more solemn in Latin"
"what's gone is gone"
"good-bye"
"I could sure use a drink"

"give me a call"
"which bus goes downtown"
"I'm going this way"
"we're not"

An Opinion on the Question of Pornography

THERE'S NOTHING more debauched than thinking.
This sort of wantonness runs wild like a wind-borne weed
on a plot laid out for daisies.

Nothing's sacred for those who think.
Calling things brazenly by name,
risqué analyses, salacious syntheses,
frenzied, rakish chases after the bare facts,
the filthy fingering of touchy subjects,
discussion in heat—it's music to their ears.

In broad daylight or under cover of the night
they form circles, triangles, or pairs.
The partners' age and sex are unimportant.
Their eyes glitter, their cheeks are flushed.
Friend leads friend astray.
Degenerate daughters corrupt their fathers.
A brother pimps for his little sister.

They prefer the fruits
from the forbidden tree of knowledge
to the pink buttocks found in glossy magazines—
all that ultimately simplehearted smut.
The books they relish have no pictures.
What variety they have lies in certain phrases
marked with a thumbnail or a crayon.

It's shocking, the positions,
the unchecked simplicity with which
one mind contrives to fertilize another!
Such positions the Kamasutra itself doesn't know.

During these trysts of theirs the only thing that's steamy is the tea.
People sit on their chairs and move their lips.
Everyone crosses only his own legs
so that one foot is resting on the floor,
while the other dangles freely in midair.
Only now and then does somebody get up,
go to the window
and through a crack in the curtains
take a peep out at the street.

A Tale Begun

THE WORLD is never ready
for the birth of a child.

Our ships are not yet back from Vinland.
We still have to get over the St. Gotthard pass.
We've got to outwit the watchmen on the desert of Thor,
fight our way through the sewers to Warsaw's center,
gain access to King Harold the Butterpat
and wait until the downfall of Minister Fouché.
Only in Acapulco
can we begin anew.

We've run out of bandages,
matches, hydraulic presses, arguments, and water.
We haven't got the trucks, we haven't got the Mings' support.
This skinny horse won't be enough to bribe the sheriff.
No news so far about the Tartars' captives.
We'll need a warmer cave for winter
and someone who can speak Harari.

We don't know who to trust in Nineveh,
what conditions the prince cardinal will decree,
which names Beria's still got inside his files.
They say Charles the Hammer strikes tomorrow at dawn.
In this situation let's appease Cheops,
report ourselves of our own free will,
change faiths,
pretend to be friends with the Doge
and that we've got nothing to do with the Kwabe tribe.

Time to light the fires.
Let's send a cable to grandma in Zabierzów.
Let's untie the knots in the yurt's leather straps.

May delivery be easy,
may our child grow and be well.
Let him be happy from time to time
and leap over abysses.
Let his heart have strength to endure
and his mind be awake and reach far.

But not so far
that it sees into the future.
Spare him
that one gift,
O heavenly powers.

Into the Ark

AN ENDLESS rain is just beginning.
Into the ark, for where else can you go:
you poems for a single voice,
private exultations,
unnecessary talents,
surplus curiosity,
short-range sorrows and fears,
eagerness to see things from all six sides.

Rivers are swelling and bursting their banks.
Into the ark: all you chiaroscuros and halftones,
you details, ornaments, and whims,
silly exceptions,
forgotten signs,
countless shades of the color gray,
play for play's sake,
and tears of mirth.

As far as the eye can see, there's water and a hazy horizon.
Into the ark: plans for the distant future,
joy in difference,
admiration for the better man,
choice not narrowed down to one of two,
outworn scruples,
time to think it over,
and the belief that all of this
will still come in handy some day.

For the sake of the children
that we still are,
fairy tales have happy endings.
That's the only finale that will do here, too.
The rain will stop,
the waves will subside,
the clouds will part
in the cleared-up sky,
and they'll be once more
what clouds overhead ought to be:
lofty and rather lighthearted
in their likeness to things
drying in the sun—
isles of bliss,
lambs,
cauliflowers,
diapers.

Possibilities

I PREFER movies.
I prefer cats.
I prefer the oaks along the Warta.
I prefer Dickens to Dostoyevski.
I prefer myself liking people
to myself loving mankind.
I prefer keeping a needle and thread on hand, just in case.
I prefer the color green.
I prefer not to maintain
that reason is to blame for everything.
I prefer exceptions.
I prefer to leave early.
I prefer talking to doctors about something else.
I prefer the old fine-lined illustrations.
I prefer the absurdity of writing poems
to the absurdity of not writing poems.
I prefer, where love's concerned, nonspecific anniversaries
that can be celebrated every day.
I prefer moralists
who promise me nothing.
I prefer cunning kindness to the over-trustful kind.
I prefer the earth in civvies.
I prefer conquered to conquering countries.
I prefer having some reservations.
I prefer the hell of chaos to the hell of order.
I prefer Grimm's fairy tales to the newspapers' front pages.
I prefer leaves without flowers to flowers without leaves.
I prefer dogs with uncropped tails.
I prefer light eyes, since mine are dark.
I prefer desk drawers.
I prefer many things that I haven't mentioned here
to many things I've also left unsaid.
I prefer zeroes on the loose
to those lined up behind a cipher.
I prefer the time of insects to the time of stars.
I prefer to knock on wood.
I prefer not to ask how much longer and when.
I prefer keeping in mind even the possibility
that existence has its own reason for being.

Miracle Fair

THE COMMONPLACE miracle:
that so many common miracles take place.

The usual miracle:
invisible dogs barking
in the dead of night

One of many miracles:
a small and airy cloud
is able to upstage the massive moon.

Several miracles in one:
an alder is reflected in the water
and is reversed from left to right
and grows from crown to root
and never hits the bottom
though the water isn't deep.

A run-of-the-mill miracle:
winds mild to moderate
turning gusty in storms.

A miracle in the first place:
cows will be cows.

Next but not least:
just this cherry orchard
from just this cherry pit.

A miracle minus top hat and tails:
fluttering white doves.

A miracle (what else can you call it):
the sun rose today at three fourteen A.M.
and will set tonight at one past eight.

A miracle that's lost on us:
the hand actually has fewer than six fingers
but still it's got more than four.

A miracle, just take a look around:
the inescapable earth.

An extra miracle, extra and ordinary:
the unthinkable
can be thought.

The People on the Bridge

AN ODD PLANET, and those on it are odd, too.
They're subject to time but they won't admit it.
They have their own ways of expressing protest.
They make up little pictures, like for instance this:

At first glance, nothing special.
What you see is water.
And one of its banks.
And a little boat sailing strenuously upstream.
And a bridge over the water, and people on the bridge.
It appears that the people are picking up their pace
because of the rain just beginning to lash down
from a dark cloud.

The thing is, nothing else happens.
The cloud doesn't change its color or its shape.
The rain doesn't increase or subside.
The boat sails on without moving.
The people on the bridge are running now
exactly where they ran before.

It's difficult at this point to keep from commenting:
This picture is by no means innocent.
Time has been stopped here.
Its laws are no longer consulted.
It's been relieved of its influence over the course of events.
It's been ignored and insulted.

On account of a rebel,
one Hiroshige Utagawa
(a being who, by the way,
died long ago and in due course),
time has tripped and fallen down.

It might well be simply a trifling prank,
an antic on the scale of just a couple of galaxies,
let us however, just in case,
add one final comment for the record:

For generations, it's been considered good form here
to think highly of this picture,
to be entranced and moved.

There are those for whom even this is not enough.
They go so far as to hear the rain's spatter,
to feel the cold drops on their necks and backs,
they look at the bridge and the people on it
as if they saw themselves there
running the same never-to-be-finished race
through the same endless, ever-to-be-covered distance,
and they have the nerve to believe
that this is really so.

Jerzy Ficowski
1924–

I'll Tell You a Story

I'LL TELL you a history, a story
before it comes up clean
with our human grit
carefully removed
well preserved
like pterodactyl bones
beneath the gobi desert

I'll tell it to you warm
from auschwitz ovens
I'll tell to you cold
from kolyma snows
a story of dirty hands
a story of hands chopped off

you won't find it in textbooks
it would stain
the blank spaces
on the map of time and times

I'll tell you a story
the unwritten the indescribable one
which occasionally comes
to watch the exhuming of dreams
in proof I have silence
shot straight through
that's why I'm whispering
I'll tell you a history, a story

But don't repeat it

How to Spoil Cannibals' Fun

FOR A LONG time I've been
wondering how to spoil
cannibals' fun

wait until they
bake themselves
beneath the golden lid of the sun
but the cooking would just
toughen them up

not let them
eat you
the program holds no food for thought
and is not entirely realistic
when
they've got you on
the tip of their tongues

eat them
how tasteless

then perhaps
turn them off people
how rude

so they sit
in their comfortable jungles
bursting with
humanity

Basis for Division

HE HAD only words
they twisted his words
behind his back
tongue-tied he took part
in a division
fair as an ax
the handle to the executioner
to the victim the blade
He wanted to ask
on what basis
but the basis was
a stump for his neck
the stump was already used to it
a tree had been
cut off it once

Ex-Jewish Things

SHE'S GOT a wardrobe from which
the dresses managed to escape
they would have gone out of style anyway

an armchair from which
somebody once got up
just for a moment
that lasted the rest of his life

pots and pans full of hunger
but handy when
you want to eat your fill

portrait of a murdered girl
in living color

she could also have gotten a black table
good condition
but she didn't like its looks

sad somehow

Thomases

I KEEP coming across Thomases
faithful
to their steadfast ignorance
with their hands in their pockets

they don't want to hurt
their pain-free fingers
with someone else's wounds

in their palms
they clutch their own
snug touch

their measured
pulses
pound nails
pound nails
into our crosses
and coffins

From the History of Journalism

THE NAMELESSLY dead
the meticulously murdered
on ghetto sidewalks
were covered with newspapers
until they were carted off

newspapers since then
with increasing circulation
have diligently served
to cover up the truth
that's lying spread-eagled on its back

as long as it's not breathing
and doesn't raise its head
otherwise the swarming letters
the blowflies, the fleshflies of words
would rise up buzzing from the startled sheets
in search of other prey

Zbigniew Herbert
1924–

Mr. Cogito's Soul

IN THE past
we know from history
she would go out from the body
when the heart stopped

with the last breath
she went quietly away
to the blue meadows of heaven

Mr. Cogito's soul
acts differently

during his life she leaves his body
without a word of farewell

for months for years she lives
on different continents
beyond the frontiers
of Mr. Cogito

it is hard to locate her address
she sends no news of herself
avoids contacts
doesn't write letters

no one knows when she will return
perhaps she has left forever

Mr. Cogito struggles to overcome
the base feeling of jealousy

He thinks well of his soul
thinks of her with tenderness

undoubtedly she must live also
in the bodies of others

certainly there are too few souls
for all humanity

Mr. Cogito accepts his fate
he has no other way out

he even attempts to say
—my own soul mine

he thinks of his soul affectionately
he thinks of his soul with tenderness

> therefore when she appears
> unexpectedly
> he doesn't welcome her with the words
> —it's good you've come back

> he only looks at her from an angle
> as she sits before the mirror
> combing her hair
> tangled and gray

Translated by John Carpenter
and Bogdana Carpenter

Mr. Cogito—the Return

1

MR. Cogito
has made up his mind to return
to the stony bosom
of his homeland

the decision is dramatic
he will regret it bitterly

but no longer can he endure
empty everyday expressions
—comment allez-vous
—wie geht's
—how are you

at first glance simple the questions
demand a complicated answer

Mr. Cogito tears off
the bandages of polite indifference

he has stopped believing in progress
he is concerned about his own wound

displays of abundance
fill him with boredom

he became attached only
to a Dorian column
the Church of San Clemente
the portrait of a certain lady
a book he didn't have time to read
and a few other trifles

therefore he returns
he sees already
the frontier
a plowed field
murderous shooting towers
dense thickets of wire

soundless
armor-plated doors
slowly close behind him

and already
he is
alone
in the treasure-house
of all misfortunes

2

so why does he return
ask friends
from the better world

he could stay here
somehow make ends meet

entrust the wound
to chemical stain remover

leave it behind in waiting rooms
of immense airports

so why is he returning

—to the water of childhood
—to entangled roots
—to the clasp of memory
—to the hand the face
seared on the grill of time

at first glance simple the questions
demand a complicated answer

probably Mr. Cogito returns
to give a reply

to the whisperings of fear
to impossible happiness
to the blow given from behind
to the deadly question

*Translated by John Carpenter
and Bogdana Carpenter*

Mr. Cogito and the Imagination

1

MR. Cogito never trusted
tricks of the imagination

the piano at the top of the Alps
played false concerts for him

he didn't appreciate labyrinths
the Sphinx filled him with loathing

he lived in a house with no basement
without mirrors or dialectics

jungles of tangled images
were not his home

he would rarely soar
on the wings of a metaphor
and then he fell like Icarus
into the embrace of the Great Mother

he adored tautologies
explanations
idem per idem

that a bird is a bird
slavery means slavery
a knife is a knife
death remains death

he loved
the flat horizon
a straight line
the gravity of the earth

2

Mr. Cogito will be numbered
among the species *minores*

he will accept indifferently the verdict
of future scholars of the letter

he used the imagination
for entirely different purposes

he wanted to make it
an instrument of compassion

he wanted to understand to the very end

—Pascal's night
—the nature of a diamond
—the melancholy of the prophets
—Achilles' wrath
—the madness of those who kill
—the dreams of Mary Stuart
—Neanderthal fear
—the despair of the last Aztecs
—Nietzsche's long death throes
—the joy of the painter of Lascaux
—the rise and fall of an oak
—the rise and fall of Rome

and so to bring the dead back to life
to preserve the covenant

Mr. Cogito's imagination
has the motion of a pendulum

it crosses with precision
from suffering to suffering

there is no place in it
for the artificial fires of poetry

he would like to remain faithful
to uncertain clarity

*Translated by John Carpenter
and Bogdana Carpenter*

Mr. Cogito on Virtue

1

IT IS NOT at all strange
she isn't the bride
of real men

of generals
athletes of power
despots

through the ages she follows them
this tearful old maid
in a dreadful hat from the Salvation Army
she reprimands them

she drags out of the junkroom
a portrait of Socrates
a little cross molded from bread
old words

—while marvelous life reverberates all around
ruddy as a slaughterhouse at dawn

she could almost be buried
in a silver casket
of innocent souvenirs

she becomes smaller and smaller
like a hair in the throat
like a buzzing in the ear

2

my God
if she was a little younger
a little prettier

kept up with the spirit of the times
swayed her hips
to the rhythm of popular music

maybe then she would be loved
by real men
generals athletes of power despots

if she took care of herself
looked presentable
like Liz Taylor
or the Goddess of Victory

but an odor of mothballs
wafts from her
she compresses her lips
repeats a great—No

unbearable in her stubbornness
ridiculous as a scarecrow
as the dream of an anarchist
as the lives of the saints

Translated by John Carpenter
and Bogdana Carpenter

The Divine Claudius

IT WAS said
I was begotten by Nature
but unfinished
like an abandoned sculpture
a sketch
the damaged fragment of a poem

for years I played the half-wit
idiots live more safely
I calmly put up with insults
if I planted all the pits
thrown into my face
an olive grove would spring up
a vast oasis of palms

I received a many-sided education
Livy the rhetoricians philosophers
I spoke Greek like an Athenian
although Plato I recalled
only in the lying position

I completed my studies
in dockside taverns and brothels
those unwritten dictionaries of vulgar Latin
bottomless treasuries of crime and lust

after the murder of Caligula
I hid behind a curtain
they dragged me out by force
I didn't manage to adopt an intelligent expression
when they threw at my feet the world
ridiculous and flat

from then on I became the most diligent
emperor in universal history
a Hercules of bureaucracy
I recall with pride
my liberal law
giving permission to let out
sounds of the belly during feasts

I deny the charge of cruelty often made against me
in reality I was only absentminded

on the day of Messalina's violent murder—
the poor thing was killed I admit on my orders—
I asked during the banquet—Why hasn't Madame come
a deathly silence answered me
really I forgot

sometimes it would happen I invited
the dead to a game of dice
I punished failure to attend with a fine
overburdened by so many labors
I might have made mistakes in details

it seems
I ordered thirty-five senators
and the cavalrymen of some three centurions
to be executed
well what of it
a bit less purple
fewer gold rings
on the other hand—and this isn't a trifle—
more room in the theater

no one wanted to understand
that the goal of these operations was sublime
I longed to make death familiar to people
to dull its edge
bring it down to the banal everyday dimension
of a slight depression or runny nose

and here is the proof
of my delicacy of feeling
I removed the statue of gentle Augustus
from the square of executions
so the sensitive marble
wouldn't hear the roars of the condemned

my nights were devoted to study
I wrote the history of the Etruscans
a history of Carthage
a bagatelle about Saturn
a contribution to the theory of games
and a treatise on the venom of serpents

it was I who saved Ostia
from the invasion of sand
I drained swamps
built aqueducts
since then it has become easier
in Rome to wash away blood

I expanded the frontiers of the empire
by Brittany Mauretania
and if I recall correctly Thrace

my death was caused by my wife Agrippina
and an uncontrollable passion for boletus
mushrooms—the essence of the forest—became the essence of death

descendants—remember with proper respect and honor
at least one merit of the divine Claudius
I added new signs and sounds to our alphabet
expanded the limits of speech that is the limits of freedom

the letters I discovered—beloved daughters—Digamma and Antisigma
led my shadow
as I pursued the path with tottering steps to the dark land of Orkus

Translated by John Carpenter and Bogdana Carpenter

The Monster of Mr. Cogito

1

LUCKY Saint George
from his knight's saddle
could exactly evaluate
the strength and movements of the dragon

the first principle of strategy
is to assess the enemy accurately

Mr. Cogito
is in a worse position

he sits in the low
saddle of a valley
covered with thick fog

through fog it is impossible to perceive
fiery eyes
greedy claws
jaws

through fog
one sees only
the shimmering of nothingness

the monster of Mr. Cogito
has no measurements

it is difficult to describe
escapes definition

it is like an immense depression
spread out over the country

it can't be pierced
with a pen
with an argument
or spear

were it not for its suffocating weight
and the death it sends down
one would think
it is the hallucination
of a sick imagination

but it exists
for certain it exists

like carbon monoxide it fills
houses temples markets

poisons wells
destroys the structures of the mind
covers bread with mold

the proof of the existence of the monster
is its victims

it is not direct proof
but sufficient

2

reasonable people say
we can live together
with the monster

we only have to avoid
sudden movements
sudden speech

if there is a threat
assume the form
of a rock or a leaf

listen to wise Nature
recommending mimicry

that we breathe shallowly
pretend we aren't there

   Mr. Cogito however
   does not want a life of make-believe

   he would like to fight
   with the monster
   on firm ground

   so he walks out at dawn
   into a sleepy suburb
   carefully equipped
   with a long sharp object

   he calls to the monster
   on the empty streets

   he offends the monster
   provokes the monster

   like a bold skirmisher
   of an army that doesn't exist

   he calls—
   come out contemptible coward

   through the fog
   one sees only
   the huge snout of nothingness

      Mr. Cogito wants to enter
      the uneven battle

it ought to happen
possibly soon

before there will be
a fall from inertia
an ordinary death without glory
suffocation from formlessness

Translated by John Carpenter
and Bogdana Carpenter

Damastes (Also Known as Procrustes) Speaks

MY MOVABLE empire between Athens and Megara
I ruled alone over forests ravines precipices
without the advice of old men foolish insignia with a simple club
dressed only in the shadow of a wolf
and terror caused by the sound of the word Damastes

I lacked subjects that is I had them briefly
they didn't live as long as dawn however it is slander
to say I was a bandit as the falsifiers of history claim

in reality I was a scholar and social reformer
my real passion was anthropometry

I invented a bed with the measurements of a perfect man
I compared the travelers I caught with this bed
it was hard to avoid—I admit—stretching limbs cutting legs
the patients died but the more there were who perished
the more I was certain my research was right
the goal was noble progress demands victims

I longed to abolish the difference between the high and the low
I wanted to give a single form to disgustingly varied humanity
I never stopped in my efforts to make people equal

my life was taken by Theseus the murderer of the innocent Minotaur
the one who went through the labyrinth with a woman's ball of yarn
an impostor full of tricks without principles or a vision of the future

I have the well-grounded hope others will continue my labor
and bring the task so boldly begun to its end

Translated by John Carpenter and Bogdana Carpenter

The Power of Taste

For Professor Izydora Dąmbska

IT DIDN'T require great character at all
our refusal disagreement and resistance
we had a shred of necessary courage
but fundamentally it was a matter of taste
                              Yes taste
in which there are fibers of soul the cartilage of conscience

Who knows if we had been better and more attractively tempted
sent rose-skinned women thin as a wafer
or fantastic creatures from the paintings of Hieronymus Bosch
but what kind of hell was there at this time
a wet pit the murderers' alley the barrack
called a palace of justice
a home-brewed Mephisto in a Lenin jacket
sent Aurora's grandchildren out into the field
boys with potato faces
very ugly girls with red hands

Verily their rhetoric was made of cheap sacking
(Marcus Tullius kept turning in his grave)
chains of tautologies a couple of concepts like flails
the dialectics of slaughterers no distinctions in reasoning
syntax deprived of beauty of the subjunctive

So aesthetics can be helpful in life
one should not neglect the study of beauty

Before we declare our consent we must carefully examine
the shape of the architecture the rhythm of the drums and pipes
official colors the despicable ritual of funerals

    Our eyes and ears refused obedience
    the princes of our senses proudly chose exile

It did not require great character at all
we had a shred of necessary courage
but fundamentally it was a matter of taste
                              Yes taste
that commands us to get out to make a wry face draw out a sneer
even if for this the precious capital of the body the head
                              must fall

Translated by John Carpenter and Bogdana Carpenter

Report from a Besieged City

TOO OLD TO carry arms and to fight like others—

they generously assigned to me the inferior role of a chronicler
I record—not knowing for whom—the history of the siege

I have to be precise but I don't know when the invasion began
two hundred years ago in December in autumn perhaps yesterday at
    dawn
here everybody is losing the sense of time

we were left with the place an attachment to the place
still we keep ruins of temples phantoms of gardens of houses
if we were to lose the ruins we would be left with nothing

I write as I can in the rhythm of unending weeks
monday: storehouses are empty a rat is now a unit of currency
tuesday: the mayor is killed by unknown assailants
wednesday: talks of armistice the enemy interned our envoys
we don't know where they are being kept i.e. tortured
thursday: after a stormy meeting the majority voted down
the motion of spice merchants on unconditional surrender
friday: the onset of plague saturday: the suicide of
N.N., the most steadfast defender sunday: no water we repulsed
the attack at the eastern gate named the Gate of the Alliance

I know all this is monotonous nobody would care

I avoid comments keep emotions under control describe facts
they say facts only are valued on foreign markets
but with a certain pride I wish to convey to the world
thanks to the war we raised a new species of children
our children don't like fairy tales they play killing
day and night they dream of soup bread bones
exactly like dogs and cats

in the evening I like to wander in the confines of the City
along the frontiers of our uncertain freedom
I look from above on the multitude of armies on their lights
I listen to the din of drums to barbaric shrieks
it's incredible that the City is still resisting

the siege has been long the foes must replace each other
they have nothing in common except a desire to destroy us
the Goths the Tartars the Swedes the Emperor's troupes regiments of
Our Lord's Transfiguration
who could count them
colors of banners change as does the forest on the horizon
from the bird's delicate yellow in the spring through the green the red
    to the winter black

and so in the evening freed from facts I am able to give thought
to bygone faraway matters for instance to our
allies overseas I know they feel true compassion
they send us flour sacks of comfort lard and good counsel
without even realizing that we were betrayed by their fathers
our former allies from the time of the second Apocalypse
their sons are not guilty they deserve our gratitude so we are grateful
they have never lived through the eternity of a siege
those marked by misfortune are always alone
Dalai Lama's defenders Kurds Afghan mountaineers

now as I write these words proponents of compromise
have won a slight advantage over the party of the dauntless
usual shifts of mood our fate is still in the balance

cemeteries grow larger the number of defenders shrinks
but the defense continues and will last to the end
and even if the City falls and one of us survives
he will carry the City inside him on the roads of exile
he will be the City

we look at the face of hunger the face of fire the face of death
and the worst of them all—the face of treason

and only our dreams have not been humiliated

Warsaw 1982
Translated by Czesław Miłosz

Transformations of Livy

How DID they understand Livy my grandfather my great grandfather
certainly they read him in high school
at the not very propitious time of the year
when a chestnut stands in the window—fervent candelabras of blooms—
all the thoughts of grandfather and great grandfather running breathless
  to Mizia
who sings in the garden shows her décolletage also her heavenly legs up
  to the knees
or Gabi from the Vienna opera with ringlets like a cherub
Gabi with a snub nose and Mozart in her throat
or in the end to kindhearted Józia refuge of the dejected
with no beauty talent or great demands
and so they read Livy—O season of blossoms—
in the smell of chalk boredom naphthalene for cleaning the floor
under a portrait of the emperor
because at that time there was an emperor
and the empire like all empires
seemed eternal

Reading the history of the City they surrendered to the illusion
that they are Romans or descendants of the Romans
these sons of the conquered themselves enslaved
surely the Latin master contributed to this
with his rank of Court Councillor
a collection of antique virtues under a worn-out frock coat
so following Livy he implanted in his pupils the contempt for the mob
the revolt of the people—*res tam foede*—aroused loathing in them
whereas all of the conquests appeared just
they showed simply the victory of what is better stronger
that is why they were pained by the defeat at Lake Trasimeno
the superiority of Scipio filled them with pride
they learned of the death of Hannibal with genuine relief
easily too easily they let themselves be led
through the entrenchments of subordinate clauses
complex constructions governed by the gerund
rivers swollen with elocution
pitfalls of syntax
—to battle
for a cause not theirs

Only my father and myself after him
read Livy against Livy
carefully examining what is underneath the fresco
this is why the theatrical gesture of Scaevola awoke no echo in us
shouts of centurions triumphal marches
while we were willing to be moved by the defeat
of the Samnites Gauls or Etruscans
we counted many of the names of peoples turned to dust by the Romans
buried without glory who for Livy
were not worth even a wrinkle of style
those Hirpins Apulians Lucanians Osunans
also the inhabitants of Tarentum Metapontum Locri

My father knew well and I also know
that one day on a remote boundary
without any signs in heaven
in Pannonia Sarajevo or Trebizond
in a city by a cold sea
or in a valley of Panshir
a local conflagration will explode

and the empire will fall

Translated by John Carpenter and Bogdana Carpenter

The Adventures of Mr. Cogito with Music

1

LONG ago
actually since the dawn of his life
Mr. Cogito surrendered
to the tantalizing spell of music

he was carried through the forests of infancy
by his mother's melodious voice

Ukrainian nurses
hummed him to sleep
a lullaby spread wide as the Dnieper

he grew
as if urged on by sounds
in chords
dissonances
vertiginous crescendos

he was given a basic
musical education
not complete to be sure
a First Piano Book
(part one)

he remembers hunger as a student
more intense than the hunger for food
when he waited before a concert
for the gift of a free ticket

it is difficult to say when
he began to be tormented
by doubts
scruples
the reproach of conscience

he listened to music rarely
not voraciously as before
with a growing feeling of shame

the spring of joy had dried up

it was not the fault
of the masters
of the motet
the sonata
the fugue

the revolutions of things
fields of gravitation
have changed
and together with them
the inner axis
of Mr. Cogito

he could not
enter the river
of earlier rapture

2

Mr. Cogito
began to collect
arguments against music

as if he intended to write
a treatise on disappointed love

to drown harmony
with angry rhetoric

to cast his own burden
onto the frail shoulders of the violin

a hood of anathema
over the clear face

    but let us think about it impartially
    music
    is not without fault

    its inglorious beginnings—
    sounds in intervals
    drove workers on
    wrung out sweat

    the Etruscans flogged slaves
    to the accompaniment of pipes and flutes

    and therefore
    morally indifferent
    like the sides of a triangle
    the spiral of Archimedes
    the anatomy of a bee

    it abandons the three dimensions
    flirts with infinity
    places ephemeral ornaments
    over the abyss of time

    its obvious and hidden power
    caused anxiety among philosophers

    the godlike Plato warned—
    changes in musical style

provoke social upheavals
the abolition of laws

gentle Leibniz consoled
that nevertheless it provides order
and is a hidden
arithmetic
training
of the soul

but what is it
what is it really

—a metronome of the universe
—the exaltation of air
—celestial medicine
—a steam whistle of emotion

3

Mr. Cogito
suspends without answer
reflexions on the essence of music

but the tyrannical power of this art
does not leave him in peace

the momentum with which it forces
its way into our interior

it makes us sad without any reason
it gives us joy with no cause

it fills harelike hearts
of recruits with the blood of heroes

it absolves too easily
it purifies free of charge

—and who gave it the right
to wrench us by the hair
to wring tears from the eyes
to provoke us to attack—

Mr. Cogito
who is condemned to stony speech
grating syllables
secretly adores
volatile light-mindedness

the carnival of an island and groves
beyond good and evil

the true cause of the separation
is incompatibility of characters

different symmetry of the body
different orbits of conscience

Mr. Cogito
always defended himself
against the smoke of time

he valued concrete objects
standing quietly in space

he worshiped things that are permanent
almost immortal

dreams about the speech of cherubs
he left in the garden of dreams

he chose
what depends
on earthly measures and judgment

so when the hour comes
he can consent without a murmur

to the trial of truth and falsehood
to the trial of fire and water

Translated by John Carpenter
and Bogdana Carpenter

The Buttons

In memoriam Captain Edward Herbert

ONLY THE buttons were relentless
survived and now turn up Unbent
eyewitnesses to buried crimes
The mass grave's only monument

They'll testify and God will count them
He'll take pity on their toil
But how can they be freed in flesh
from this dank resisting soil

A bird flies by A cloud sets sail
A leaf drifts down The mallows bloom
Silence in the heavens while
the Smolensk forest exhales gloom

And only the relentless buttons
still sounding voice of silenced swarms
the buttons the unyielding bones
of overcoats and uniforms

Wiktor Woroszylski

1927–

Philately

I REMEMBER philately
from childhood Has anyone noticed
that the philately of our childhood years
is gone I don't want
to sound like some old-timer who keeps repeating
I remember when and *It's all gone* But
what can you do when the great hunts the adventure those little
boys collecting chance are really gone
chance a shimmering patch
of ocean an island's
crooked neck happiness a guttural
grunt an oddity a piece of
the world's jigsaw puzzle which turned out
differently for each of us We used to chase
after that gaudy narcotic we
swapped we bought it for pennies
in dark little shops we kept lookout you had to watch
your jungle like a hawk Drive
imagination dreams all that
used to form an open world for which
I uncertain of my motives
am ashamed to yearn now that
there is another philately of closed
systems to which
one buys an entrance pass Anyone
may subscribe and at the designated
time receive the same segments
of the collection that every other subscriber
gets The bounds
are known No
daring no chance In their place
organization and specialization those forces
of the modern world It is

a total philately It imparts
perhaps other pleasures Sense of belonging
symmetry completion counting as one
of the stamp-collecting industry's consumers certainty
of getting the same as the rest in one's chosen
field of surfaces pasted
as agreed I can't
say anything against it since that's
the way it is I'll just say
that it was something completely
different which
no longer is and will never be again

Fascist Nations

SHORTLY after the war of 1914–1918 the first fascist nations
emerged in Europe In those nations
the sun rose and set at the usual time shedding light
on homestead roofs and hills' green slopes Cattle
mooed gently in cowsheds Mothers kissed
their children's foreheads to wake them at dawn Fathers returning from
    work
with cheerful weariness in their bones smelled
the smoke from their hearths and after dinner
fell asleep in armchairs or tinkered intrepidly or
practiced their music with a passion Children
played at stickball at hopscotch and hide-and-seek Little girls
sprouted breasts and overnight
little girls turned into big girls filled with whisper
and murmur like trees in the woods and sudden giggles the sound of
    which
made boys' throats go dry On summer evenings
curtains lit from within showed shadows meeting
parting and meeting again tenderly Whereas in winter
lovers inhaled the steam of each other's breath in snowy gardens And
one might also mention cats arching their backs sparrows
soaring up above the pavement old women on their porches flowers cut
    and potted nurses
taking patients' temperatures people sweeping streets
with brooms One might mention drying

wood wind in a thicket damp furrows in a field And one might also
call to mind many particulars bearing witness that

For there were no signs on the sky mournful comets
burning bushes water turned to blood For
life went on as always Hence there truly were in those nations
many ordinary people and good people and people
who knew nothing and to whom
it never occurred and who
didn't consider themselves accessories and who
had nothing to do with it and who didn't
even read the papers or read them carelessly caught up
in thoughts of what they had to get done
fix the leaking roof get the shoes
repaired propose have
a beer mix the paint light a candle and who
really didn't see the fear in a neighbor's eyes didn't
hear the trembling in travelers' voices asking the way didn't
see the difference didn't hear
an inner voice or if
they had their doubts there was nothing they could do and they took
  comfort
saying At least we
aren't doing anything wrong we live the way we always did Which was
  true

And yet these were
fascist nations

Indictment

HOW UGLY this man is
with his disfigured face With his eyelid
half-covering his eye
like a curtain that got stuck
With a gag of blood on his lips

His ugliness
is subversive Even on flat ground
his legs give way beneath him

The broken line of his arms
lifts a hand
against the arrow-straightness of your rifles, your salutes

Nothing speaks in his favor
He's backed
only by the wall

He doesn't even speak up for himself
He's mute He won't

Your Honor, Humanity sir:
His sweaty shirt
is an enemy flag
His foul breath
poisons the atmosphere
His sadness assaults
the serenity of his fellowmen

It's obvious that
for this obstinate sticking to ugliness
the man deserves to be forgotten
by those who live in beauty

*   *   *

IN THIS slough becoming stone
of our muffled daily war,
in this press, in this embrace—
I've never been so free before

Beneath the puddle's skin of scum
where creatures stir a murky floor,
with my torn lip, with my salt wound—
I've never been so free before

Pierced with a hiss, with the monstrous nail
of a dark star's driving force,
in this abasement and amazement—
I've never been so free before

Where the tram tracks twist in nooses,
where the square lies bruised and sore,
in this trap of threadbare beauty—
I've never been so free before

For everything turns into freedom
when slavery's conquest is complete:
earth's heavy breath, the screams of stones,
the flood of filth beneath our feet

Then, the sunflower's restive turning,
your restless sleep, your mind's quick pace—
everything turns into freedom,
every key releases space

And life will break through shells and shadows
to show its bright uncovered face—
each thing we touch unleashes us
and turns to freedom on such days

1977

Roommates

THE ROOMMATES I had in my hospital bed
were very nice people
                    But now they are dead

Mr. Wiśniewski in the bed on my left
who had one lung removed and believed
that the other one had only to learn
how to breathe and he wouldn't wheeze

Mr. Liebchen in the bed on my right
who was ashamed of being bedridden
and fed with a spoon, and also of the tube that
ran from his blanket to a see-through bottle, and who told us
how he'd been driving his truck for two solid days

Mr. Jastrzębski in the opposite bed
who cracked jokes Doctor why don't you just admit
that in my gut there's a monster with pincers
rhymes with "answer," get it, doc?

I remember things about them And I remember
myself with them For example once
all day I told them stories from the books of a certain writer
who had just been denounced by the party paper
And they listened transfixed
It wasn't long ago But now they're dead

Only Mr. Wasilewski from the bed by the window
is still alive I see him from time to time by my house
and we stop for a minute His heart still bothers him
but he's back to work I guess it pays
(he says) to stick it out till I retire

Well and I'm alive

The Padlock Speaks
(From the sequence "Diary of Internment, II")

WAKE UP I'm your morning bird
my tender rasping rubs your eyes
my rusty rays illuminate your prayers

You've been a good boy Now you may take a step
but be careful I can jam at any time
Don't make my gravity any harder than it is
after all I'm only iron and can barely hold my own

Today I have to hear your confession
dictate your letter home
count your movements and your glances
make sure nothing's been concealed

Learn how to read me my dear scholar
this will help you make it through another day

And don't let your dream try to escape

The Belly of Barbara N.
(From the "Diary of Internment, II")

IN THIS DARK warm shelter
with its vault carefully shaped
from the flesh and blood of this young woman
he's hiding
from the padlock's hoarse pursuit
from the yellow sign barring the way
from the preying pitfall of despair
from the glowing cinder tip of hatred
he the prisoner waiting to be born
conceived between his father's release
and the arrest of his mother
not entered on the list of internees
the future citizen and soldier of this country

What a Poem Is Allowed
(From the "Diary of Internment, II")

POEM BE careful
there are some things you can't do

You may
writhe in pain
gnash your teeth in shame
remember evil

You may not
make a note of someone's kindness
well-wishing
help

Kindness will be branded
well-wishing will be punished
The one who helped
will be betrayed
and perish helplessly

Tadeusz Nowak

1930–

Psalm on a Dumpheap

HOPES FAITHS philosophies
tossed on the trash heap doused
with gas for the holocaust
Hopes faiths philosophies
sprinkled with quicklime to prevent
spreading of pestilence and plague

Hopes faiths philosophies
explained in books or else engraved in bronze
beside a dirt road where a goat
an ox a peasant woman trudge
and time like a mutt with one maimed paw
leaves its whimpering trace along the sand

Hopes faiths philosophies There
where the drowning man clutches at straws
where peasants ride the sunrise bareback
where a god descending from three nails
devours a lamb's living innards
where the dawn's grain trickles
through a library chopped to chaff

Hopes faiths philosophies
trash thrown in the river's flesh
manure carried to the new-plowed field
a book of genesis nailed
to the outhouse wall Above the orchards
stars wheel through its pages

Pastoral Psalm
For Zosia

WHERE ARE you Beyond the water
beyond the quiet grass
where the rustling treetops write
their letters meant for us
where knives aren't used for cutting
not even cutting bread
where the only thing that's shut in
is a hedge-rimmed flowerbed

Where are you Beyond terror
beyond the spider and the mouse
where burdock ears and radar
have trouble hearing us
where money isn't minted
as the hammers pound
where thunderbolts sleep peacefully
beside a rusty mound

Where are you Beyond yourself
beyond your dream and song
where not a single blade of grass
is overlooked for long
where you can say "I am"
and forget you ever saw
a white hen's neck beneath an ax
a birch beneath a saw

Psalm with No Answer

WHO FALLS in love who weeps
who is led through the psalter
who's had enough of sweets
and dogs barking over the water

Who has eyes of green
whom has the green grown over
whose summer dream are you in
my Slavic myth angel and lover

Who saddles his horse by night
who mounts his horse in pain
who sees the crowned eagle in flight
while power dawns over the plains

Who's set drunk by hope
and whom has terror fed
whose neck is hugged by the rope
and the arms of the Trojan dead

Who's lost his memory here
who lays his memory bare
whose shattered loins reveal
sweet marrow of a prayer

Asian Prayer XI

I FEAR MY dream It scares me
with its wide black-ringed eyes
Some say that they are stones
embalmed in glacial ice

Totalitarian chunks of cold
push terminal moraines
We'll glaze in them like mammoths
stuffed with moss hunger and pain

Beside us birds frozen in flight
uneaten dogs cats and mice
A stunted cross beams blessings
in frigid northern lights

I fear my dream It scares me
Dream tell me what is your name:
Samoyed? Nenets? reindeer?
Come huddle close to my flame

And you come closer brother Rus
who fought in the great war
and took home just a box of nails
to mend a pigsty door

I'll go to sleep beside you
while your pulse beats in my veins
until the glacier buries us
in terminal moraines

Devil's Prayer II

I LIE HERE Buried With me lie
Babylon Greece Byzantium Rome
I lie here Buried Up above me
the Mongol dawn of Genghis Khan
galloping through the rampant grass
with disemboweled corpses strapped
like booty to its matted mane
I lie here And beside me lie
Franz Wilhelm and Czar Nicholas
Lord summon from my memory
their nooses jails two-headed eagles
and cast them up against your autumn sky

I lie here Buried The earth is thick
with folk laments Forefathers' Eves
peasant revolts the church the hovels
the Bible and Das Kapital
the party the police stool pigeon Pete
axes knives hammers ropes oak stakes
while up above our Popiełuszko
shines brighter than the morning star
A mouse pops up his only witness
and brings him from the autumn fields
a grain of millet a tiny icicle of grief

I lie here Buried I'm pierced through
by aspen stakes and silver spikes
by knives honed on a stone of stars
and on mists heavier than stone
Above me brothers drink denatured spirits
and children gnaw cheap sausages
They will leave and the lights will die

and only dogs' eyes will still glitter
Then the archangel hovering above us
will note down on his way to Babylon
the buried empires One of them is still alive

Urszula Kozioł
1931–

A Polish Lesson

To a young man

BETWEEN "I know" and "I don't know"
there's a zone of possibilities sown with safe signs
of desperation and perplexity
those safety valves or emergency doors
you force open in case of catastrophe

their curving birdlike back advises you to leave
your *i*'s undotted your *t*'s uncrossed
don't pin the fleeting
butterflies into place

learn to say "I don't know"
learn to say "I can't say" "I don't remember"
learn to say nothing

train your memory to fail
recognize that you have the right to make mistakes
to stay mute

insist that the noise in your ears is due merely
to history's winds or to the changes in pressure
that make mirages out of daily life

*   *   *

YOU LIVE by the very edges
by a wavering outline

sudden darkness
freezes
your blood

the world's maw with its black palate
is poised above you
its fang a sickle
shines indifferently

you'll die
you'll die with a poem on your lips
with a poem spoken once again
to no one

We Won't Look Truth in the Eye

TRUTH HAS no eyes
no face
no tongue

truth is wingless
it doesn't live
beyond the seven seas hills forests

I think that truth
is more like a nagging growth
that gnaws inside

I think it's
that sticky thing
rolled into a ball somewhere under your skin
it hates comfort
it suddenly swells
and sends out desperate signals
dark ones
like a deaf-mute's moving hands

it hurts
it chokes
you can't keep quiet any longer

you scream

Jan Prokop
1931–

Song of Four-Egg Enriched Ribbon Noodles

I'M ONE OF the seven maybe eight basic foodstuffs
that are always available I don't cause a stir
when I grace store shelves in Jaworzno Płock or even Ślemień in
   abundance
I take life in moderation
(its salt doesn't bite me and doesn't cheer me up)
I roll dolefully on ruddy waves of tomato soup
served to forest workers in Łopuszna
once I entertained a ranking dignitary
and his fair-haired little girl
I've also gone abroad in the trunks of Fiats
campers cook me hurriedly in Bulgaria Serbia and Slovenia
I've even been as far as Cyprus
where my corpse my little cardboard
home from which the spirit had fled (had flown away)
in the shape of countless crunchy little tongues
was found at the foot of an ancient fortress in the city of Famagusta

Song of a Crust of Bread Thrown to Sparrows on Victory Square, Formerly Saxonian Square, by the Tomb of the Unknown Soldier

I WANDERED all the way here from the town of Mielec
in the pocket of the unskilled, single cleaning woman Zofia N.
though I was born on the sunny Mazovian plains
for which the poet Broniewski bard of the Revolution yearned
Our bus came on a no-work Saturday
people pressed their noses to shop windows
Zofia N. was after children's tights and diapers
since she's the unwed mother of eight-month-old Mariusz

Dear Mr. Comrade Chairman Sir
she'd written for the umpteenth time
please cast your kind consideration on my unfavorable conditions
I live in a kitchen I'd like a housing allocation
Having bitten out the soft part smeared with lard
she held me with her fingers with the same uncertain air
she'd had when Zdzisław S. the deputy director locked
the office door behind him and offered her the vodka
But when she heard the sudden order for the changing of the guard
she started and I fell softly to the stones
of that square so full of history and suffering
that when the birds' hard beaks hit me
I thought: these must be eagles fleeing abandoned banners

Ernest Bryll

1935–

Soot

THE SOOT keeps drifting everywhere,
It gives the walls their grayish color,
It's scrubbed each day from off your collar
And combed, like old age, from your hair.

You scrape the blackened windowsill
And paint it bright time and again,
You rub your body raw in vain
And try to bleach the laundry clean

Sometimes a cinder in your lid
Will force an unexpected tear:
The hurt eye, suddenly washed clear,
Sees beauty—or comes close to it . . .

The Charge

WE RUSHED to work, our heads hunched over,
Through a smoky mist that stank of sulphur.
A tram rang in the distance. We were wet
From drizzling rain, and being late, and sweat.
Our nylon coats, inflated by the wind,
Rose up behind each back like angry wings—

The force of charging hussars, raging angels' wrath
Compelled us and we cleared a path
So fiercely that the ground beneath us shook
And no one dared to stop us, dared to look . . .

Then suddenly the tram arrived. Once we climbed in,
a crush of bodies pinned our feathers to our skin.

Only late arrivals hanging outside on the steps
Kept their wings, wind-blown, majestic, and wet.

In a Fever

I DREAMED that in a light-industry mill
Where tired women choke and cough up dust
One worn-out woman failed her masters' trust.
She couldn't stick it out to closing time—
It's rough but then the pay's not bad, and still
When the night shift's done you can stand in line,
Then get the kids to school with what they need—
Instead she broke down, and began to bleed.
Her white twill shirt turned red. Her piercing scream
Burst the factory gates, and in my dream
A horde of women poured into the street.

It overflowed, and no one dared to meet
Them face to face, though Warsaw phone calls warned
That this must stop . . .
                    The local party hacks
Sank clutching their receivers, drowned
In human seas. One of them yelled: "Hand out some meat,
And then remind these gals to watch their step,
Families can get hurt, better turn back
Now." Others whispered to the guards who kept
Watch over Them, the nation's true elite:
"Don't sweat, boys. It's just women. Running scared.
They're old and ugly, too. We couldn't care
Less . . ."
            It was true. Their hair was gray with grime,
Their faces worn and wrinkled, and their weary
Bodies had paid the price of working overtime.

When they finally came in range, then you could see
That those who yelled at you, yelled toothlessly . . .

No, better wake up. Now. Before a terse
Voice gives the order no one can reverse.

6 April 1986

Leszek A. Moczulski
1938–

Report

THE EXPANSIVE language of my childhood. And
then this dry and businesslike voice.
A brand-new housing project, badly lit. Evening. People. A taxi stop.
Some sort of fight. Someone being chased. Someone runs away.
And this voice slams up against the high-rise windows:
"Sic 'em!"
Like a terse report.
A briefing on the world. A summary.
"Sic 'em!"
The voice is like a report.
And man is like a dog.

From "Words of Welcome"

HISTORY'S PIECE of paper, I observed, looked like others written in
    such situations,
but the man who read it out loud stuttered, garbled the text, corrected
    himself:
this time he was reading the truth.

*

I thought I wouldn't have to learn contempt
but a certain kind of lie, elusive at first,
drives me to these extremes.

*

The techniques of destruction:
sarcasm, servile distortions, an exaggerated style,
derision, precise definitions replaced by epithets,
hatred urging us toward emptiness.

Sooner or later, an arid silence invades
the lips that employ these techniques.

*

They excite themselves with their own lie,
only multiplied by many mouths.

*

They talk about tragedy
to conceal their crime
thus further reserving their right
to criminal errors.

From "Ordinary Poems"

I PRAISE the Singer sewing machine,
the bread it bought, and my father's hands
moving from it to my head on Sunday morning.
Father's forty years drowned in it as if it were a sea,
the forty stubborn years of a man
slowly moving toward
the salt and truth of life.
It bought bread and whatever I needed to live
in holiday bliss.
Father spent his nights
talking and singing with it.
Final truth flows from it
in the unremitting music
of the people who make objects
to repudiate terror.
It challenged the contempt
bred by a man-made night.
It flashed and passed like the man
who flashed and passed
as he used it to work
toward the world's becoming
in one of a thousand workshops.
It flashed and passed.
An echo. A memory. A grain.

A joy not paid for.
Probably at sunrise on the sea.
I praise the Singer sewing machine—
its needle, shuttle, sheave, and belt—
                              all final.

Ryszard Krynicki
1943–

The Heart

WHERE ARE you tearing off to, my poor heart,

as if you were still looking for
your incarnation?

1973/1977

On the Eve

ON THE EVE of the First of May,
coming home from work along gray Red Army Street
I was just going by a butcher's window,
when I caught from the corner of my eye
how among imitation and original pieces
of motionlessly lurking meat
all of a sudden
a fairly hairy hand
with a gold ring on the middle finger
and fingernails polished red
moved slightly.

And nothing happened.

I Don't Know

I DON'T KNOW if the poet
can really be impartial
like a doctor who treats
two bitter enemies the same,

since he has to take sides
as only a sister of mercy can,
patient witness

to a patient's pain

July 1977

You Don't Have To

YOU DON'T have to look,
they turn up by themselves, the slaves,
ready to wield the power
that only

love or fatal sickness
has over us

1977

Maybe It's You

AT LAST I'm on an equal
footing; I'm always pressed
for time; I commute
up to my ears in debt; in a crowded bus
maybe it's you who hates

some sort of me?

I'll Remember That

REMEMBER
I'm your friend:

you can tell me everything.

And you can tell me everything, too.

I'll remember that,
stone.

                                        25 July 1977

If It Comes to Pass

IF IT COMES to pass that I have to shout
"Long live Poland!"

—what language will I have to do it in?

                                        1975

Rose

MANIFEST mystery, simple labyrinth,

careless, immortal,
ill-boding rose, I don't want to yet,

I don't have the right yet to die.

                                        28 June 1974

The Answer

AFTER A TALK with my would-be publisher
I myself don't know
who's the author of my book.

(The state, the paper allocations, the moon's pull,
or other circumstances?)

It'll only be half an answer:
The author of my book

is the Polish language

1973/1975

Almost All

IT'S THE twentieth century, so
I go to bed with the newspaper,
my glasses, pills, and wristwatch
are within reach;
I don't know if I'll fall asleep,
I don't know if I'll wake up,

that's all

December 1977

Socialist Realism

THE GHOST of the dove of peace
with a little white flag in its beak
flies to and fro
along the Berlin Wall.
A sniper
keeps it in his sights.

A New Day

THE VETERANS' Cooperative "Twenty Years of People's Poland"
waits for a new office, the wind blows,
the Holocene sands grind, hair falls out.
Your unemployed you
passes by a line that grows before your eyes near a newsstand.
A crumpled paper
with an already faded photo of the new leader
takes flight and falls beneath the wheels
of an ambulance. Open,
open the cablegram with the pink ribbon,
maybe the cobalt helped.
When you take your child to the kindergarten
in a postwar barrack, you'll see, as on any other day,
the guard on the wall
who doesn't take his eyes

off whatever's going on on the other side.

September 1980

I Am Not Worthy

LORD, I AM not worthy
of Thy punishment
but if it is to fall,
let it strike only me.
Forgive me, I have sinned grievously even now,
by believing you would hold me, too,
in your all-and-nothing seeing

gaze.

Do Not Want to Die for Us

DO NOT WANT to die for us,
do not want to live for us:

live with us.

Sleep Well

SLEEP well,
the devil keeps watch:
he eavesdrops and spies
on our most secret fears and dreams,
trying to learn something new

from us, too.

Suddenly

MY LITTLE GIRL, my great teacher
(who nobly forgives me my errors, since
she knows already that even spelling rules change)
shouts in triumph from her room: "The mantis
devours its mate only in human
captivity."

So What If

SO WHAT if
we were right,

dragonflies from before the ice age?

I Can't Help You

POOR MOTH, I can't help you,
I can only turn out the light.

Yes, She Says

YES, I survived.
Now I face an
equally serious challenge: to get
on a bus,
to get home.

You're Free

"YOU'RE free," says the guard,
and the iron gate shuts

this time from this side.

A Stop

DURING an endless stop
in East Berlin
a young customs officer zealously unscrews
the tin ceiling
in the car's corridor; standing on tiptoe,
he checks for runaways; the top of his uniform
pulls up and reveals a plump
helpless tummy, cuddling

a holster.

Facing the Wall

A WOMAN turns the mirror around
to face the wall: now the wall
reflects the dead snow
crunching under iron soles.
The fire freezes.
Nothingness puts on its bayonets.

From a Window

THE SOLDIERS kill
boredom; they have brown shoes
and to the mute question "What did you do,
when they ordered you to shoot defenseless people?"
they have a mute answer: "I was lucky,
I was just guarding the TV transmitter."

The Wall

LOOKING at the concrete wall,
the barbed wire and the steel gate,
for a minute I couldn't remember
my country's other names: a little door
in the gate half-opened
—but it was just a guard who came out,
then disappeared into a nearby store.

Ewa Lipska
1945–

From the Gulf Stream of Sleep

NATIONS run out of trains
onto the icy steppes of air
of frozen years.

With barbed-wire stars
overhead.

Seven-year-olds
learn by heart
the sums of dreams.

The conductor's voice
rips the world
from the Gulf Stream of sleep:
AUSSTEIGEN!
VYKHODIT'!

Silence
stamps its feet
for warmth.

Envoy

TO WRITE so that a beggar
would take it for money.

And the dying
would take it for birth.

Dictation

PAY ATTENTION to dictation.
Don't make a mistake.
Don't crowd the letters
in nation.
Know
when to open and when to close
the parentheses of lips.
Silence—
starts with what letter?
Decline
but not in every case.
Be careful
not to divide love in two
as in black currant or first comer.
Take care
to place a period after certain dates.
After others
a pause.
See that you don't
abbreviate life.

Remember
not to misspell death.
Die
correctly.

* * *

FLOODS didn't save me
though I've already been at the bottom.

Fires didn't save me
although I've been burning for years.

Accidents didn't save me
though cars and trains ran me over.

I wasn't saved by the planes
that exploded with me in midair.

The walls of great cities
fell upon me.

Poisonous mushrooms didn't save me
or the well-aimed shots of firing squads.

The end of the world didn't save me:
it didn't have time.

Nothing saved me.

I'M ALIVE.

Questions at a Poetry Reading

YOUR favorite color?
Your luckiest day?
A poem that lay beyond your grasp?
You don't have any hope?
You frighten us.
Why a black sky
or time shot down?
An empty hand, a hat that floats across the sea?
Why a wedding dress
with a funeral wreath?
Hospital halls
instead of garden paths?
Why not the future? Why the past?
Do you believe? You don't believe?

You frighten us.
We run from you.

I try to restrain them.
They're running into the flames.

My Loneliness

MY LONELINESS finished Valedictorians' School.
It's punctual and hardworking.
It's been given orders and awards.

My loneliness
is peopled.
Several thousand readers walk across it.
It's been written down.
Crossed out.

It's tired of ruling
like Frederick the Great.

It's starting to have its disciples.
Its timid slaves.

My loneliness is public.
It lies at the bottom of the cage
with its silent flight feathers
plucked out.

An Attempt

WHEN WE tried to talk to one another
it turned out
that we had different languages.
Just as we began to speak
a common tongue
they took our speech away.
As we descended from the hills
we shared only
the shadows of the dead.

The Wall

ON THE RIGHT side of the wall
wooden platforms.
Polyglot rustle of words.
Shoals of tourists.
We hold binoculars to our eyes.
To our eyes
magnifying the situation.
In the situation brought up close.

On the left side of the wall
an ordinary human hand
holds a sandwich.
It's lunchtime.
I see:
a machine gun set aside
an ordinary human face
the tired gray of eyes
aimed at the distance.
I see:
magnified air
the city's swollen edge
blushing flags
a green lettuce leaf
falling from the hand
flies up and down
tries to escape
fights with the wind
which pins it to the barbed-wire coils.
A brown German shepherd
with a pink German tongue
pretends to take a nap
in the watchful fur of the air.
The guards
brush crumbs from their uniforms.
Through binoculars
they watch our hands eyes tongues
the magnified time
on someone's watch.

On the right side of the wall
another bus drives up.

A little red-haired girl stands on tiptoe.
Someone spits out a cherry pit.
Someone bursts out laughing.
Someone's heavy silence.
Tiny leaves of fear.

History's great pageant
in the open
air.

To Marianne Büttrich

FOR A YEAR now I've been trying
to write you a letter.
But
the locusts of my thoughts
are untranslatable.

The people on duty are untranslatable
guarding my words and grammar.

My hours can't be translated
into yours.

The black lilacs behind the window.
The unbuttoned gates. The yellowed cigarette butt of a day.
The dead eye in the peephole
at six A.M.

Rilke is untranslatable too.
Die Blätter fallen, fallen . . .
Wir alle fallen . . .

I've got so much to tell you
but
a tunnel is approaching
my delayed train.

A long whistle sounds.

I'm tired, Marianne,
I'm leaving for the Bermuda Triangle
to take a rest.

Adam Zagajewski
1945–

Plans, Reports

FIRST THERE are plans
then reports
This is the language
we know how to communicate in
Everything must be foreseen
Everything must be
confirmed later
What really happens
doesn't attract anyone's attention

Fire

PROBABLY I am an ordinary middle-class
believer in individual rights, the word
"freedom" is simple to me, it doesn't mean
the freedom of any class in particular.
Politically naive, with an average
education (brief moments of clear vision
are its main nourishment), I remember
the blazing appeal of that fire which parches
the lips of the thirsty crowd and burns
books and chars the skin of cities. I used to sing
those songs and I know how great it is
to run with others; later, by myself,
with the taste of ashes in my mouth, I heard
the lie's ironic voice and the choir screaming
and when I touched my head I could feel
the arched skull of my country, its hard edge.

Translated by Renata Gorczynski

Iron

WHY IT HAS to be December.
The dark doves of snow fly,
falling on the slabs of the sidewalk. What is
talent against iron, what is
thought against a uniform, what is music
against a truncheon, what is joy against
fear, the dark heavy snow encloses
the sprouts of the dream, from a balcony you notice
as young Norwid shows his ID
to the police and he pleads
he cannot sign the volkslist, the patrolmen
laugh with contempt, they have snorting
nostrils and red-hot cheeks,
tormentors hired from the scenes
of the Passion, what's that silent crowd
in a blue streetcar against them,
who's that sad girl, is that the way
the new epoch begins, is this tank
with a long Gogolian nose its godfather,
and that gritting iron weighing down
the delicate dove of snow,
will it seal the Declaration
of Loyalty and mortally wound
the freedom song, meanwhile you notice
as young Norwid, released by
the snorting nostrils and blood-red
cheeks, is hiding in a gateway, he,
exactly like you, is as breakable
as a record, and
the passersby—each of them carrying a handful
of infinity—all
are rounded up, all are frozen,
the cobblestone wavers under the tank treads
of decrees. At night you ask me,
desperate, what to do; why, I wonder,
has your concept proven false
or the hoop of your imagination snapped, no,
only iron has swollen.

Translated by Renata Gorczynski

The Trial

ONE PROSECUTOR (bald, speaks in low voice,
stammering), three judges (that one
on the right plays with the glasses
belonging to the one who sits
in the middle), three bearded defendants
(exchanging smiles with the audience),
three attorneys (white hair, memo books,
gowns hemmed with a thin stripe of green),
three lies, two semitruths, one
justice (nonattendant, without excuse),
outside the window a rook polishes its eternal gown.
The woman clerk yawns. The judge, that one who
sits on the left, counts nonexistent
trees on a dusty wall. Boredom
rhymes with itself, as if it were
a physical person. The prosecutor lashes
the memory of the defendants, what does it mean
in the face of oblivion, whose being
the court has forgotten. Someone weeps and some stifled
reality, pale like the shoots of winter
potatoes, germinates again.
The judge, a tailor with the qualities of a demiurge,
still ponders openly and secretly
how many years he'll cut down his own and those three lives,
the common divine rosy fire-resistant life.

Translated by Renata Gorczynski

Flag

IN THE morning I wake and try to check
with opera glasses
what kind of flag is waving over my city
Black white or ash-colored like fear
Or has my city already been conquered
or is it still defending itself or begging
the conquerors for understanding or
wearing mourning after several seconds

of oblivion or perhaps I myself am
the flag only I can't
see it just as I can't see
my own heart

Translated by John Carpenter

Thorns

IF, ALSO, the dictators wanted
to read our bitter, furious, and
thoroughly worked-out poems, then poetry
certainly would change the world. But
roses, too, do not know the poems devoted
to them. Thorns don't drink blood.

Translated by John Carpenter

Brevier

ALL THE GREAT events of yours,
blows struck without notice,
victorious battles waged
against your own brothers
—you have already conquered steel mills and mines,
broken in the doors of our
apartments: go further, now
arrest thoughts—they will grow smaller
and smaller until they become the size of brevier,
the tiny print in footnotes to the poems of Norwid.

Translated by John Carpenter

A Polish Dictionary

LANCES, banners, sabers, horses.
Horses, razors, alphabet blocks,
warm green lamps, women, manners, burning
conversations, and the yellow ashes of the books.
A real lady prays only in French.
Over an étagère, a swarthy Tatar Madonna,
immobile, like a hummingbird.
A huge family reunion. The children are sent
to the garden. Vodka bitter as wormwood
and the Old Testament of jokes. A shrill
eternity of laughter. Apples and cherries.
Bread. Take it all away from them.
It's nothing, a Mediterranean of trivia,
an ordinary life with its taste of water.
Take away suspenders, shoelaces,
belts, ink, and pens,
linen, paper, iron.
Take away their eyes and their tongues.
They'll become valiant as bronze and steel.

Translated by Renata Gorczynski

He Acts

HE ACTS, in splendor and in darkness,
in the roar of waterfalls and in the silence of sleep,
but not as your well-protected shepherds
would have it. He looks for the longest line,
the road so circuitous
it is barely visible, and fades away
in suffering. Only blind men, only
owls feel sometimes its dwindling trace
under their eyelids.

Translated by Renata Gorczynski

Lightning

WE LIVED understanding little and craving
knowledge. As plants do, when they grow toward
light, we sought justice
and we found it only in the plants,
in the leaves of the horse chestnut, enormous
as oblivion, in the fern shrubs which swayed
slowly and made no promises.
In silence. In music. In a poem. We sought
justice, confusing it with beauty.
Emotion is governed by strict laws.
We turned our backs on cruelty
and boredom. There's no solution, that much
we knew, there are only fragments, and the fact that
we spoke in complete sentences seemed to us
a strange joke. How easy it was to hate
a policeman. Even his face seemed to us
a part of his uniform. The errors of others
were easy to detect. On a hot day, the river
reflected mountains, clouds. Life then was
round like a balloon when it gets going.
Spruces stood still, filled with shadows
and stillness like the depths of an ocean. Green
eyes, your wet skin,
my lizard. In the evening, mute lightning
flickered in the sky. It was other people's thoughts
burning down safety. One had to
pack in a hurry and go farther,
east or west, mapping out
an escape route.

Translated by Renata Gorczynski

My Masters

MY MASTERS are not infallible.
They're neither Goethe,
who had a sleepless night
only when distant volcanoes moaned, nor Horace,
who wrote in the language of gods
and altar boys. My masters
seek my advice. In fleecy
overcoats hurriedly slipped on
over their dreams, at dawn, when
the cool wind interrogates the birds,
my masters talk in whispers.
I can hear their broken speech.

Translated by Renata Gorczynski

To Go to Lvov

TO GO TO Lvov. Which station
for Lvov, if not in a dream, at dawn, when dew
gleams on a suitcase, when express
trains and bullet trains are being born. To leave
in haste for Lvov, night or day, in September
or in March. But only if Lvov exists,
if it is to be found within the frontiers and not just
in my new passport, if lances of trees
—of poplar and ash—still breathe aloud
like Indians, and if streams mumble
their dark Esperanto, and grass snakes like soft signs
in the Russian language disappear
into thickets. To pack and set off, to leave
without a trace, at noon, to vanish
like fainting maidens. And burdocks, green
armies of burdocks, and below, under the canvas
of a Venetian café, the snails converse
about eternity. But the cathedral rises,
you remember, so straight, as straight
as Sunday and white napkins and a bucket
full of raspberries standing on the floor, and
my desire which wasn't born yet,

only gardens and weeds and the amber
of Queen Anne cherries, and indecent Fredro.
There was always too much of Lvov, no one could
comprehend its boroughs, hear
the murmur of each stone scorched
by the sun, at night the Orthodox church's silence was unlike
that of the cathedral, the Jesuits
baptized plants, leaf by leaf, but they grew,
grew so mindlessly, and joy hovered
everywhere, in hallways and in coffee mills
revolving by themselves, in blue
teapots, in starch, which was the first
formalist, in drops of rain and in the thorns
of roses. Frozen forsythia yellowed by the window.
The bells pealed and the air vibrated, the cornets
of nuns sailed like schooners near
the theater, there was so much of the world that
it had to do encores over and over,
the audience was in frenzy and didn't want
to leave the house. My aunts couldn't have known
yet that I'd resurrect them,
and lived so trustfully, so singly;
servants, clean and ironed, ran for
fresh cream, inside the houses
a bit of anger and great expectation, Brzozowski
came as a visiting lecturer, one of my
uncles kept writing a poem entitled *Why*,
dedicated to the Almighty, and there was too much
of Lvov, it brimmed the container,
it burst glasses, overflowed
each pond, lake, smoked through every
chimney, turned into fire, storm,
laughed with lightning, grew meek,
returned home, read the New Testament,
slept on a sofa beside the Carpathian rug,
there was too much of Lvov, and now
there isn't any, it grew relentlessly
and the scissors cut it, chilly gardeners
as always in May, without mercy,
without love, ah, wait till warm June
comes with soft ferns, boundless
fields of summer, i.e., the reality.

But scissors cut it, along the line and through
the fiber, tailors, gardeners, censors
cut the body and the wreaths, pruning shears worked
diligently, as in a child's cutout
along the dotted line of a roe deer or a swan.
Scissors, penknives, and razor blades scratched,
cut, and shortened the voluptuous dresses
of prelates, of squares and houses, and trees
fell soundlessly, as in a jungle,
and the cathedral trembled, people bade good-bye
without handkerchiefs, no tears, such a dry
mouth, I won't see you anymore, so much death
awaits you, why must every city
become Jerusalem and every man a Jew,
and now in a hurry just
pack, always, each day,
and go breathless, go to Lvov, after all
it exists, quiet and pure as
a peach. It is everywhere.

Translated by Renata Gorczynski

Stanisław Barańczak
1946–

The Three Magi
To Lech Dymarski

THEY WILL probably come just after the New Year.
As usual, early in the morning.
The forceps of the doorbell will pull you out by the head
from under the bedclothes; dazed as a newborn baby,
you'll open the door. The star of an ID
will flash before your eyes.
Three men. In one of them you'll recognize
with sheepish amazement (isn't this a small
world) your schoolmate of years ago.
Since that time he'll hardly have changed,
only grown a mustache,
perhaps gained a little weight.
They'll enter. The gold of their watches will glitter (isn't
this a gray dawn), the smoke from their cigarettes
will fill the room with a fragrance like incense.
All that's missing is myrrh, you'll think half-consciously—
while with your heel you're shoving under the couch the book they
    mustn't find—
what is this myrrh, anyway,
you'd have to finally look it up
someday. You'll come
with us, sir. You'll go
with them. Isn't this a white snow.
Isn't this a black Fiat.
Wasn't this a vast world.

Along with the Dust
(From "The Housing Poems")

ALONG WITH the dust on the books,
the fingerprints on all the glass (fragile—
do not drop), along with
a ration coupon for sugar and a cross to bear
(fragile—this side up), I'm moving,
along with the writing in my lap, the thousands
of terms in my head (fragile—remember with care),
with an extra thousand zlotys just in case
(fragile—do not worry too much), along with a mask of self-confidence
and a wound in my back, along with an empty promise and an ill-
fitting hope (fragile—do not trust), along
with maybe finally and quick hurry up,
along with you can depend on it and I'm sick to death
(fragile—do not die), along with let's begin at the beginning
and knock on wood and what's the use,
and along with this love that's
all that will stay with me for better, for worse,
and forever, it's fragile, you movers,

and it's all a lot heavier than it looks

To Grażyna

TO REMEMBER about the cigarettes. So that they're always at hand,
ready to be slipped into his pocket, when they take him away once again.

To know by heart all the prison regulations about parcels and visits.
And how to force the facial muscles into a smile.

To be able to extinguish a cop's threatening yell with one cold glance,
calmly making tea while they eviscerate the desk drawers.

To write letters from a cell or a clinic, saying that everything's OK.

So many abilities, such perfection. No, I mean it.
If only in order not to waste those gifts,
you should have been rewarded with immortality
or at least with its defective version, life.

Death. No, this can't be serious, I can't accept this.
There were many more difficult things that never brought you down.
If I ever admired anybody, it was you.
If anything was ever permanent, it was that admiration.
How many times did I want to tell you. No way. I was too abashed
by the gaps in my vocabulary and the microphone in your wall.
Now I hear it's too late. No, I don't believe it.

It's only nothingness, isn't it. How could a nothing like that
possibly stand between us. I'll write down, word for word and forever,
that small streak in the iris of your eye, that wrinkle at the corner
    of your mouth.
All right, I know, you won't respond to the latest postcard I sent you.
But if I'm to blame anything for that, it will be something real,
the mail office, an air crash, the postal censor.
Not nonexistence, something that doesn't exist, does it.

Don't Use the Word "Exile"

STAND WITH both feet on the solid ground of this moment
when the paved street runs up aslant and then it strikes and stings your
    soles,
and, slowing down, with a thud of sneakers inside your high-school
    briefcase,
you swerve toward the curb (those three, exactly three steps),
as the streetcar goes on, dragging and grinding, dark-green,
along the tangential curve of the tracks, beyond the corner of
    Mielżyńskiego and Fredry.

Hold on stubbornly with the whole surface of your palm to the door
    handle
of the Nojewo railway station, in the summer that smells of rain and cow
    dung,
don't lose your grip on its stout, cylindrical wood, made smooth by local
    hands,
grasp it again and again, feel its looseness and springy resistance.

And don't use the word "exile," because it's improper and senseless.
The matter can be looked at from two points of intensive view.
Either no one shoved you aside from the cobblestones on which
you are still running, in an instant that has lasted until now,

no one wrenched the door handle away from your hand that seized it
for a second, forever, and you are still there.
Or you yourself left them behind, selfishly forsaken
even as you set foot on the curb or entered the station,
because with every moment one chooses another life.

A Second Nature

AFTER A COUPLE of days, the eye gets used
to the squirrel, a gray one, not red as it should be,
to the cars, each of them five feet too long,
to the clear air, against which glistens the wet paint
of billboards, puffy clouds, and fire-escape ladders.

After a couple of weeks, the hand gets used
to the different shape of the digits one and seven,
not to mention skipping diacritical marks in your signature.

After a couple of months, even the tongue knows
how to curl in your mouth the only way that produces a correct *the*.
Another couple of months and, while tying your shoelace in the street,
you realize that you're actually doing it just to tie your shoelace,
and not in order to routinely check
if you're not followed.

After a couple of years, you have a dream:
you're standing at the kitchen sink in the forest cottage near Sieraków,
where you once spent vacation, a high-school graduate unhappily in love;
your left hand holds a kettle, your right one reaches for the faucet knob.
The dream, as if having hit a wall, suddenly stops dead,
focusing with painful intensity on a detail that's uncertain:
was that knob made of porcelain, or brass?
Still dreaming, you know with a dazzling clarity that everything depends
    on this.
As you wake up, you know with equal clarity you'll never be able to
    make sure.

After Gloria Was Gone

AFTER SEVERAL hours' showing off, the hurricane figured out
that it makes no sense to perform on three channels at once
as a whistling background for interviews with a local mayor
from another disaster area, disrupted by dog-food commercials,
and, at the same time, to put on a live show in our street.
So much work for nothing? Behind our windowpane, crossed aslant
with tape, we waited for the wind to get disheartened,
to go on strike, to leave for the north, toward New Hampshire.
The door opens to the smell of ozone, wet leaves, and safe adventure.
We stop by the knocked-down maple tree that snapped the electric line
while falling across the street in front of Mrs. Aaron's house.
Tapping her cane and still looking not that old,
almost like the time when, because she was blond,
the nuns were willing to hide her, Mrs. Aaron walks around and
    calculates
the repair costs. On the nearby sidewalk, Mr. Vitulaitis
examines the tree trunk thoughtfully, volunteers his help
and electric saw for tomorrow, those years of practice in the taiga
will come in handy, he jokes. Crushing sticks that lie on the asphalt,
here comes the pickup truck of the new neighbor, what's his name,
is it Nhu or Ngu, who brakes close to the tree and gets out,
surely without recalling the moment when, on the twenty-ninth day,
their overcrowded boat was found by the Norwegian freighter.
In something like a picnic mood, we all share comments and jokes
about the disaster. After all, it wasn't so fierce
as the forecasts had warned, no big deal, no big scars;
the harm it did to us is a reparable one, and tomorrow,
first thing in the morning, there'll be another expert visit
from the electrician, the sunrise, the insurance inspector.
It's time to go back home, remove the crosses
of tape from our windows, though we can't do the same
to our pasts or futures which have been crossed out
so many times. "The so-called pranks of nature,"
Mrs. Aaron sums up disdainfully, and she adds
that whoever is interested may inspect the devastation—
as far as she's concerned, she's going in to make some coffee.

Setting the Hand Brake

IN AN EMPTY suburban parking lot, setting the hand brake,
he wonders what it actually was that brought him here
and why on earth he was never able not to succumb
to the clichés of sorrow, familiar to all who practice
the invisible craft of exile. There always will be a homeland
of asphalt under the chilly streetlamps, a homeland of rusty crossties
under a pair of rails, which likewise can count on meeting
in infinity only; a homeland that comes along and apart,
that rushes forward with him in the canyons of floorboard cracks
and lights in strangers' windows, and his veins, and trajectories
of galactic explosion. What is it that still holds him here,
pins him down, encloses him in the circumference
of this and not another skin, planet, suburban parking lot.
And whence this arrogated, arrogant right to exile,
as if it weren't true that no one will fall asleep tonight
on his own Earth. There will be a homeland somewhere: an involuntarily
    chosen
second of awakening in motion, in the middle of a breathless whisper
a comma placed by chance, by mistake, for the time being, forever.

Julian Kornhauser
1946–

Barricade

SO MANY things, all that's left of our sagacity.
Ash-gray wardrobes, beds, an old-time Magnavox
with a missing bottom, grandfather clocks, rolled
carpets, an Infant Jesus, a stuffed hawk
marked "Baltic Seashore Souvenir," broken
chairs and prams, piles of books,
memoirs, newspapers. This mammoth heap of
revolution shrinks some every day. Someone carries
off a camp bed on the sly, aging yellow sets
of the *Illustrated News* disappear, children help themselves
to bright tin boxes, pale locksmiths
with the Infant Jesuses beneath their arms burst
breathless into the nearest yard, where the dye
of wet banners stinks. Next day
in tiny apartments dirty hawks
turn up on TV tops, and mothers lose themselves
in histories of the All-Russian
Communist (Bolshevik) Party.

Fundamental Difficulties

WHAT IS A poem a simple thought's cradle
a yellow castle on an unseen hill
a soiled sheet of paper snatched up by the wind
what is a poem memory's rubber stamp
an ordnance map a hurried breath
a senseless moment's glimmer
I really don't know
I don't know if poems are still deathless
if they help you live

Splendid Facades

OUR MEMBERS are all right
they pay their dues
they participate
they don't shirk their voluntary labor
true there are cases of splendid facades
behind which hardened egos hide
but petty egoism plays no part
in our daily party life
one comrade went to the local board
and threatened to return his party card in protest
he hadn't been promoted in three years and he
couldn't get his child into a preschool
the comrade left after a brief explanation of the mistakes
in his position
when good work proves impossible as the result of poor organization
people's aspirations are deflected from society's common goals

A Weaver

SHE IS AND will always be a weaver
it's the only work she knows or wants to know
only these legs
the bones in her feet got twisted
arched like spurs and they hurt
always piecework
three shifts at the power loom
from the time she was fifteen
up to now
angel food cake on the table
homemade leftover from the birthday party
she's got a little time now since the sick leave
some problems with the spine regretfully

It All Depends on the Individual

PEOPLE HAVE achieved a higher level
the machinist says
in the past if there was a shortage or something didn't work
they blamed the state the government
but now they see it all depends on the individual
because if an apartment house has crooked walls
or the furniture falls apart
it's not the state's fault after all
but the fault of the person who produced them

May Day Grandstand

THE LEGS hide
behind red cloth

the toil-worn
wiry
farmer-worker legs

we can only see busts
swarthy mighty
bursting with pride

while the legs
rest silently

the crowd's condemned
to only half a joy
the marchers' legs are on parade
but the other legs
seem mysterious and strange
they come from another world

if placed on public exhibition
they would emit ordinary happiness

down there though
they're up to something
they're scheming

1982

Piotr Sommer

1948–

Problems

LATER, after such a little end of the world,
our wives have to hear it all
again, surprised why on earth
we talk so earnestly
about what any child knows although
he doesn't say it. So obstinate,
as if we wanted them to take the blame—
as if they were the state.

In the Provinces

THE MUNICIPAL Office of Housing Development in Otwock
GREETS THE BROTHERLY PEOPLES OF SOCIALIST NATIONS
with each of forty-three letters mounted on a separate stake;
only the spaces between words don't have poles.
It's May eleventh, 1979.
The poles stuck in the grass make a pier.
The Municipal Office has been greeting the brotherly peoples for over
    three weeks
but the peoples still don't know a thing about it.

Indiscretions

WHERE ARE we? In ironies
so fleeting and unstressed
that no one gets them, in foolish punch lines
that buy off metaphysics with ridiculous
details, in Friday, which falls
on February fifth, in the mnemonics of days.

You can give an example, or take it for granted,
or take it or leave it, or take it and run.

And you still like certain words and those, pardon the expression,
sorts of syntax that act like something's holding them together.
Man is wholly held within those intermeanings,
he creeps in wherever he can see a space.

Trust Me

REALLY YOU won't find a better place
for all your makeup, even if we
see our way clear to getting some bathroom shelves
and you stop hitting the bottles with the towel—
there'll always be a thousand reasons to complain,
and a thousand bits of glass on the tile,
and a thousand new worries,
and another morning making you get up

Medicine

I SAW A REAL lemon again.
Ania brought it back from France.
She'd been wondering: come home or stay abroad?
And come to think of it, what keeps her here—
a few faces, a few words, this anxiety?
The lemon was yellow, it looked like the real thing.
You didn't have to put it in the window
to ripen alongside our pale tomatoes.
Or as we ourselves ripen
growing up and growing yellow over years.
No, it was already entirely itself
when she brought it, not even yellow, but gold,
and a little rough,
so I took it gratefully.

I want to wrap myself in the thick skin of the world,
I want to be tart, but good-tasting—
some child swallows me reluctantly
and I help to cure his cold.

1981–82

Tomasz Jastrun
1950–

Freedom

THEY BROUGHT me in
And read the number of the first and last names
Tattooed on my ID
And let me go
As if I weren't guilty
They must not have been looking
They missed the light
In my eyes
Two young rookie cops

I walked off free
Dragging the street's chains behind me

July 1982

The Pulp

THEY KEPT saying The nation's substance
Must be saved
At any cost

So they hid it
Beneath the bed and in silence
And they skirted police patrols
And certain topics

They dragged it out years later

It was a pulp
In which someone's eyeballs floated
And a gold wedding ring
From someone's finger

Smoke

As I was walking by
The prison walls today
I felt nothing

Forgive me
Since you all know that my nothing
Has its cellars attic
And chimney smoke

Looking through tin slits
You see the smoke
And the bruised blue sky
With its clotted bird

1983

Jan Polkowski
1953–

The Restaurant "Arcadia," Central Square, Nowa Huta

SECRETARY GENERAL of the All-Russian Communist Party
(the Bolsheviks) Vladimir Ilyich Lenin. Covered
with snow, the twenty-foot colossus is coming home from work
to his camp barrack. Gaunt, starved. Kept on his feet only
by the convoy guard's *goluboy* gaze. The frost thrusts its fist at him
slammed tight like white-hot, humming steppes. The polar
night strips bare. Roll call.
On the stained tablecloths
of Kolyma snow.

"Peter Followed Him from Afar"

THUS YOU have placed me
in myself that I might know You.
The wall, wire, and dogs look at You
with my eyes.

Hymn

THE PRISON window looks out on a compound.
Snow and clay surrounded
by a concrete wall and barbed wire.
What do you need (O gray eagle)
this tight crown for?

Among Us, the Unclean Ones

THEY PLAY cards at a table: the old one, skin and bones,
and a young man with a beard. A third
lies in bed and reads a book. Quiet,
a dark window, muffled talk.
From a photograph taped to the wall a young woman
with a little boy on her lap
looks at them. The child, lost in thought, doesn't recognize
his father; he has just lifted his hand (here the picture's
blurred) as if he were blessing
these three prisoners
(the Jews and the Greeks
and the entire earth).

March 1982

"My Sweet Motherland"

I WAS BORN in a train,
on a moving frontier,
a Jewish runt in the corner of a freight car,
a Polish-speaking Wehrmacht soldier
marching on Moscow,
an NKVD man of unknown descent
shooting at my ancestors: Poles,
Lithuanians, Tatars—nobles with a two-headed typhus
on their crests.
I was born on their moving graves:
in Kazakhstan, in Lithuania,
in Częstochowa, Kraków, Katyń, London.

This is my citizenship—your belly
raised
beneath your breasts (Annie, little mother).

(My invisible Motherland,
we'll be true to each other.)
It no longer matters.

* * *

YOU NEED me? You, the Great
Betrayed One?
I am here in this dirty lowland, in the midst of the shouts
of petty shopkccpcrs, inept thieves,
and cruel policemen.
With human ashes underfoot, I slapped Your face.
You did not leave me, contempt,
you did not leave me, hatred.
I have achieved you, inhuman language of the future.

Though Mortal, I Desired You

O WHITE FISH of November (the city is just now falling asleep).
Ashes of kings, smoke, stone masks of beggars
and informers (now famished time
falls asleep).
Only the wind survives, only the wind's
trunk with its bark stripped off;
sing (oh, sing,
my escape).

Bronisław Maj
1953–

* * *

EVENING behind the wall a child wails,
soothing words, a lullaby. Scraps
of talk, voices reach me through the walls:
I don't know never Mom I'm coming remember why it'll be all right

Behind all the walls of my room, behind any
walls anywhere—the talking
never stops. I don't see the faces, eyes; I hear
voices: unimaginable
ties binding each
with each, everybody, everything.
You can't pick and choose. There's no place
for a breath
faultless and free.

* * *

THESE ARE strong, calm words
when the time comes for just these people
to speak them: they say *no*, they say *enough*,
they say *shame* and *truth*. These are not
trite, funny words when spoken by
the tight-lipped men
who speak up only
then. Women listen in silence,
with suddenly idle hands,
and children, who suddenly understand
everything. And this is just what you've got
then: silent women
with hands helplessly dropped,

children, beginning to understand, words
that demand a voice, and
a low ironic laugh
the only sound.

* * *

WHO WILL BEAR witness to these times?
Who will record them? Certainly none of us:
we've lived here too long, we've soaked the epoch
up too well, we're too loyal to it to tell the truth
about it. To tell the truth—at all. Loyal:
I say *justice*, but think of revenge's dark joy,
I say *concern* while thinking *them* and *us*,
and *what have they done to me*. I've got
nothing else in my defense: loyalty. And weakness:
that I hated wicked people, cheated to shield
the truth, that scorn was my sick pride.
Hatred, scorn, lies—for so many years,
so as to survive and stay pure. But it can't be done:
survive and stay pure. At best—survive.
Stay—mute. Ask: Who will bear witness?
Knowing full well that none of us and certainly no one
else will. Hence without a word. An empty epoch.
More full of life than any other because
ours, and we won't see another. Uproar,
clamor, wail, laugh, howl, the same old
song, no words, not a single word
to speak someday
for us.

* * *

RAIN OUTSIDE a window, a glass of tea on the table,
a lamp—this is how, perhaps naively, I see you
in five, in twenty, in a hundred and twenty-five
years reading this poem: thinking of me, a man
of twenty or a hundred and twenty years ago—how

did I live? I and my age: hopelessly tired people,
a few dates, sites of defeat, names: incantations we repeated
then, with the childish hope of the living, lacking
the wisdom which time has given you who lived
after it all—after us, after all of us. There's so little
I can pass on to you, no more than anyone else. But after all
I lived and I don't want to die entirely: to remain
an everyman for you, an object of statistical
pity or disdain. What was only,
only me is outside history. So I'll tell you about me
in the only language we both understand: about the smell
of wet city dust outside the window (it had just rained), the table
pressing my elbows, the clock's tick, the taste of hot
tea, the lamp's light that hurt my eyes
while I wrote this poem—in the universal language of all
five undying
senses.

* * *

March 21, 1980, Kraków

IT TAKES JUST a few minutes: the largest market square in old
Europe, a hazy morning, the city's voices still uncertain—then:
fire, blinding yellow, shocks and stuns them: in the bank's
doorway the dealing in dollars and vodka stops, the crowd's
trembling circles converge around a man who—having chained himself
to an old pump—is burning. The smell of gas, in a flash:
clothes, then hair, shivering hands and lips: the voice,
deformed by pain, is just a scream, it will never become
a word now, the harsh brown smoke of the cast-off sacrifice
won't rise to the skies, it won't form a sign: it drifts low, disappears
devoured by the crowd's hungry lungs, which—in just a few
minutes—will choose life: in the entrance across the way the dealing
in dollars and vodka resumes, the crowd's calm circles
disperse, the last flame of
old Europe dies out, and the city's triumphant voice
grows strong: *Aflame, you never know if you're becoming
free.* And whatever is yours is
doomed.

*　*　*

May 13, 1981

THE WORLD: whole and indivisible, begins where
my hands end. As I stand at the window, I see it: the green spires
of Skałka and Wawel, the dome of St. Ann's, further, deep blue
hills, for so the woods look at dusk, beyond them
other valleys filled with cities, and still more cities:
on rivers, on wide plains sloping
to the sea, beyond which lies another sea, sharp brown
peaks, mountain passes, roads, and people's houses not unlike my
own. The breath that fills my mouth, lungs, blood is just
a share—mine only for a moment—of all the air
enveloping the world: indivisible. I see it—I know
that it is there, right at hand, at my fingertips, at my breath's warmth.
The rest is just a matter of miles, of imperfect vision—insignificant
on a scale of mind and heart. Hence right
at hand, just a few blocks off, on a large
city square full of people, my brother shoots
my father, here, at my fingertips.
Just like that: not a bang, not a whimper, like that.

*　*　*

THIS CITY died. Blue streetcars moan
on the curves, the streets can't curb
a nervous gray crowd, colored light streams from the signs. Voices,
dust, exhaust. This city died when you understood
how easily it could die. Those who think that it happens in flashes and
    claps of thunder,
as in the Scriptures, are wrong. So is the Master
who sneers that it will come on cat's paws. They are wrong
about the method. Not ready: in mid-word, with an
unsent letter, with a woman still wanting love, a hidden
sin which will stay mortal—no one is
ready. Love what is doomed. There is no other
love. Part each time as if forever,
that is, be kind, forgive. Don't put off for tomorrow,

don't keep back the great, important words, there may not be
time, or space. Henceforth there will be
no other love. This city is
everywhere.

NOTES

MIECZYSŁAW JASTRUN, "Repatriate." After 1956 thousands of Poles were at last allowed to return to their country from the Soviet Union, where they had spent years, often in concentration camps, as a consequence of the 1939 Soviet seizure of Poland's prewar eastern territories. *Vorkuta*—the site of some of the harshest hard labor camps in Siberia.

CZESŁAW MIŁOSZ, "Bypassing Rue Descartes." *Water snake*—in Lithuania, where the author grew up, many pagan beliefs survived, among them the cult of water snakes, which were associated with the sun. A strict taboo protected a water snake from any harm inflicted by man.—C.M.

"Caffé Greco." *Turowicz*—Jerzy Turowicz, editor-in-chief of the Kraków-based Catholic weekly *Tygodnik powszechny*.

WITOLD WIRPSZA, "Footnote." The poem obviously refers to Shakespeare's "Hamlet," but even more clearly to Zbigniew Herbert's famous poem "Elegy of Fortinbras."

TADEUSZ RÓŻEWICZ, "The poet grows weaker . . ." *A noir, E blanc . . .*—the opening line of Arthur Rimbaud's sonnet "The Vowels."

WISŁAWA SZYMBORSKA, "In Broad Daylight." *Baczyński*—Krzysztof Kamil Baczyński, an enormously gifted poet of the "war generation," was killed as a Home Army fighter in the Warsaw Uprising of 1944 at the age of twenty-three.

"Possibilities." *Warta*—a river in the western part of Poland.

ZBIGNIEW HERBERT, "The Buttons." *Smolensk*—the name of a Soviet city, used as a shorthand reference to the Katyń massacre, in which thousands of Polish officers, taken prisoner by Stalin's troops after the Soviet invasion of Poland in September 1939 and subsequently kept in POW camps, were summarily executed and buried.

TADEUSZ NOWAK, "Devil's Prayer II." *Forefathers' Eves*—a reference both to the pagan ritual honoring the spirits of the dead and to the masterpiece of Polish Romantic literature and theater, the drama *Dziady* (Forefathers' Eve) by Adam Mickiewicz (1798–1855).

Popiełuszko—Father Jerzy Popiełuszko, a young Warsaw priest and outspoken critic of the Communist regime, murdered by agents of the state security apparatus in 1984.

JAN PROKOP, "Song of a Crust of Bread . . ." *Victory Square*—a vast square in downtown Warsaw, with the Tomb of the Unknown Soldier serving as a site for official wreath-laying ceremonies.

Broniewski—Władysław Broniewski (1897–1962), a prominent pro-Communist poet; in postwar Poland he was made into an official cult figure.

ERNEST BRYLL, "The Charge." *Hussars*—the metaphoric imagery in this poem refers to the characteristic appearance of the *husarz*, a soldier in the legendary seventeenth-century units of heavily armed cavalry, and in particular to its most eye-catching feature: a pair of upright feathered "wings" attached to the back of the hussar's armor.

EWA LIPSKA, "From the Gulf Stream of Sleep." *Aussteigen! Vykhodit'!*—German and Russian for "Get out!"

ADAM ZAGAJEWSKI, "Iron" and "Brevier." *Norwid*—Cyprian Kamil Norwid (1821–83), a highly innovative Polish poet of the late nineteenth century, considered a spiritual father of modern Polish poetry. He was the master of an ironic but far from absurdist reflection on the meaning of history.

"To Go to Lvov." *indecent Fredro*—Aleksander Fredro (1793–1876), the most outstanding Polish comedy writer of the nineteenth century. He lived in a country estate near the city of Lvov (Polish Lwów) and his comedies had their premieres in the Lvov theater. He was also known as an author of frivolous verse.

Brzozowski—Stanisław Brzozowski (1878–1911), a great philosopher, literary critic, and novelist of the turn of the century.

STANISŁAW BARAŃCZAK, "To Grażyna." The title refers to Grażyna Kuroń, wife of the human rights activist Jacek Kuroń. Put in an internment camp for women in December 1981, she contracted a lung disease. Subsequently released, she died in a hospital in November 1982.

JULIAN KORNHAUSER, "Barricade." *histories of the All-Russian Communist (Bolshevik) Party*—the textbook by Joseph Stalin entitled *A Brief Course in the History of the VKP (B)* was required reading in the so-called ideological training sessions conducted in every workplace during the years of Stalinism in Poland.

JAN POLKOWSKI, "The Restaurant 'Arcadia' . . ." *goluboy*—Russian for "blue."

"Hymn." *gray eagle*—Poland's national emblem is a white eagle. The traditional royal crown on its head was removed after the Second World War by the regime of People's Poland and was restored only after the recent downfall of the Communist system.

" 'My Sweet Motherland.' " *Częstochowa, Kraków, Katyń, London*—Częstochowa is the location of the Holy Shrine of Virgin Mary, hence the informal religious capital of Poland; Kraków was Poland's historic capital until the seventeenth century; Katyń (see note to Herbert's "The Buttons") is a symbol of Poland's twentieth-century ordeal; and London has been the seat of the Polish government-in-exile since the Second World War.

BRONISŁAW MAJ, "It takes just a few minutes . . ." The poem's two final sentences are a quotation and a paraphrase of a fragment of a poem by Norwid (see note to Zagajewski). Indirectly, they also refer to *Ashes and Diamonds*, a novel by Jerzy Andrzejewski on which Andrzej Wajda based the script for his famous film; both the novel and the film take their titles from the same Norwid fragment.

"The world: whole and indivisible . . ." *the green spires of Skałka and Wawel*— Wawel is the ancient royal castle in Kraków; Skałka refers to the church that is part of the castle compound.

"This city died . . ." *the Master who sneers that it will come on cat's paws*— Czesław Miłosz, in his poem *"L'accélération de l'histoire."*

BIOGRAPHIES

STANISŁAW BARAŃCZAK (1946–) is a poet, essayist, critic, literary historian, and translator into Polish of Shakespeare, the English metaphysical poets, G. M. Hopkins, Emily Dickinson, Philip Larkin, James Merrill, Osip Mandelstam, Joseph Brodsky, Tomas Venclova, and other poets. In 1976 he cofounded KOR (Workers' Defense Committee) and the first uncensored literary periodical in People's Poland, the quarterly *Zapis*. Since 1981 he has lived in the United States, teaching Polish literature at Harvard University. His books in English include *Selected Poems: The Weight of the Body* (TriQuarterly Books/Another Chicago Press), *A Fugitive from Utopia: The Poetry of Zbigniew Herbert,* and *Breathing under Water, and Other East European Essays* (both Harvard University Press).

ERNEST BRYLL (1935–), a prolific poet, playwright, and fiction writer, won remarkable popularity in the 1960s by alluding in his poems and poetic plays to certain suppressed topics in Polish history and by his revival of the Romantic tradition. Though he initially supported the Communist regime, he became its opponent in reaction to the imposition of martial law. The poems included here come from his collection *Adwent* (Advent), published in 1986 by an émigré publishing house.

JERZY FICOWSKI (1924–), a poet, biographer of Bruno Schulz, and specialist in Polish Gypsy folklore, made his debut in 1948 and has since published numerous collections of poems and essays. In the late seventies he co-edited *Zapis* and was a member of KOR. His poetry combines linguistic experimentation with political and social concerns, including the fate of the Jewish community in Poland during the Holocaust. From 1977 to 1989 his collections appeared either underground or abroad.

JULIA HARTWIG (1921–) is, besides Wisława Szymborska, the most outstanding woman poet in Poland today. Since her first collection in 1956, she has published several books of poems, biographies of Apollinaire and Gérard de Nerval, and numerous translations of French and American poetry (in particular, selections of Marianne Moore and Robert Bly). Her latest collection, *Obcowanie* (Relations), published in 1987, was critically acclaimed.

ZBIGNIEW HERBERT (1924–) is, among nonémigré Polish poets, the most well known internationally. The publication of his first book was delayed by years of Stalinism during which he refused to participate in official literary life; it finally appeared in 1956. In subsequent years several more collections of his poems have appeared, each a milestone in modern Polish poetry. He is also an important playwright and essayist. Since the early seventies his poems have often employed a persona named Mr. Cogito. Herbert's collection *Raport z oblężonego miasta* (*Report from the Besieged City*, Ecco Press) published abroad and underground in 1983, is widely considered the most accomplished book of poetry produced in Poland during the years of martial law. His books in English include *Selected Poems* (Ecco Press) and a collection of essays, *Barbarian in the Garden* (Carcanet Press).

MIECZYSŁAW JASTRUN (1903–83), one of the great writers of postwar Polish literature, left behind an extensive body of work as a poet, essayist, biographer, editor, fiction writer, and translator from Russian, German, French, and other languages (his translations of Rilke, Hölderlin, and the French symbolists are especially notable). He made his debut in 1929 but reached the peak of his career in the years following the "thaw" of 1956, when his poetry, translations, and essays on the Mediterranean heritage of European culture made a considerable impact on Polish literature. His last years were marked by a deepening interest in metaphysical and religious themes.

TOMASZ JASTRUN (1950–), son of Mieczysław Jastrun, a poet and essayist, made his debut in 1978 and published several more collections before 1989, most of them underground. He was an outspoken and highly regarded poet of protest against the post-1981 "state of war" in Poland. In the late eighties he was a co-editor of the journal *Res publica*. Since 1990 he has served as cultural attaché in Sweden.

ANNA KAMIEŃSKA (1920–86), a poet, translator, critic, essayist, and editor, was the author of numerous collections of original and translated poetry (from Russian and other Slavic languages) as well as of anthologies, books for children, and collections of interpretations of poems. She was a long-time editor of the book-review section at the influential Warsaw monthly *Twórczość*. Initially a poet of peasant themes and moral concerns, she underwent a spiritual metamorphosis in the early 1970s, becoming an important poet of religious experience.

JULIAN KORNHAUSER (1946–) made his debut as a poet in 1972 and since then has published over a dozen books ranging from collections of poetry and novels to criticism and scholarly works on South Slavic literatures. He is considered a representative figure of the "Generation of '68." The controversial book of essays he coauthored with Adam Zagajewski in 1974, *Świat nie przedstawiony* (The World Not Represented), advocated a return to reality and "straightforward speaking" in Polish literature.

URSZULA KOZIOŁ (1931–), poet, fiction writer, and essayist, lives in the city of Wrocław, where she has long been the editor of the poetry section of the literary monthly *Odra*. Her first book of poems appeared in 1957. Besides several other poetry collections, she has published novels and collections of essays. Her only book in English is the recent *Poems* (Host Publications).

RYSZARD KRYNICKI (1943–), a poet and translator of German, Austrian, and English poetry, is a central figure in the "Generation of '68." He published his first two collections legally in 1969 and 1975, but from that time until the late eighties he was frequently blacklisted for political reasons and published his work, including three more books of poems, either underground or abroad. The latest phase of his career has been marked by a turn from linguistic experimentation and ornate style to moral concerns and concise, aphoristic forms. A selection of his poetry in English, *Citizen R.K. Does Not Live,* has been published by Mr. Cogito Press.

EWA LIPSKA (1945–) is one of the leading woman poets of the middle generation. In her development she has been close to the poets of the "Generation of '68," and has also been strongly influenced by Wisława Szymborska. Nine collections of her poetry have been published thus far; the latest appeared underground in 1985. *Such Times,* a selection of her poems in English, has been published by Hounslow Press.

BRONISŁAW MAJ (1953–) is, with Jan Polkowski, the most outstanding representative of the generation that entered Polish literature in the early 1980s. He made his debut in 1980 and since then has published three more books of poems. Throughout the eighties, he served as editor-in-chief of a unique, orally presented literary journal, *NaGłos,* which is now coming out in Kraków as a printed periodical.

ARTUR MIĘDZYRZECKI (1922–), married to Julia Hartwig, is a highly esteemed poet, essayist, fiction writer, and translator of Russian, French, and American poets (among others, Osip Mandelstam, Arthur Rimbaud, René Char, e. e. cummings, and William Carlos Williams). He made his debut in 1951, but his originality manifested itself fully only in the late 1960s and has shown itself most clearly in his two most recent collections, published in 1983 and 1987. He was vice-president of the Polish chapter of PEN before its dissolution by the regime in 1983, and he resumed that function with PEN's restoration in 1989.

CZESŁAW MIŁOSZ's (1911–) towering presence in contemporary Polish poetry transcends the schematic divisions between generations as well as the division between Poland-based and émigré literatures. He published his first poem in 1930 while a law student at the University of Wilno, and a year later cofounded a group of poets called Żagary. During the thirties, two books of his poems appeared. He spent the war mainly in Warsaw, where he contributed to the underground publishing network. His extensive collection of what were primarily wartime poems came out in Poland in 1945. In the next few years Miłosz worked for the new regime as cultural attaché in the United States. In 1951 he requested political asylum in Paris. During the subsequent thirty years his works were strictly banned in Poland, and the first editions of his books appeared chiefly in Paris. In 1961 he moved to California to accept a position as professor of Slavic literatures at the University of California, Berkeley. From the mid-seventies on, his poems, novels, and essays have been reprinted in Poland with increasing frequency, initially by underground presses and then, after he received the Nobel Prize for Literature in 1980, also by the official publishing houses. His work—poems as well as two novels and a dozen collections of essays—has been translated into numerous languages. The most comprehensive collection of his poetry available in English is *The Collected Poems, 1931–1987* (Ecco Press).

LESZEK A. MOCZULSKI (1938–), a poet and popular author of song lyrics, made his debut in 1971 and has published seven books of poems. Though older than most of its representatives, he has been close in his concerns and style to the "Generation of '68."

TADEUSZ NOWAK (1930–), a poet and fiction writer, is the most prominent representative of the peasant theme in Polish culture. In his poems, short stories, and lyrical novels the issue of traditional folk culture uprooted by civilization is examined in an original way. Nowak creates a multifaceted personal, cultural, and religious mythology of the rural past and juxtaposes it with modern urban experience. He published his first collection of poems in 1953 and his first collection of short stories in 1962. His most accomplished poetic work is a long series of "psalms" published in two volumes in 1971 and 1978.

JAN POLKOWSKI (1953–) is, with Bronisław Maj, the most gifted of the Polish poets who have emerged during the last decade. He made his underground debut in 1980, and his next three collections were also published underground; his first official book of poems appeared only very recently. With the imposition of martial law, he was jailed and then interned. Throughout the eighties, he co-edited what was arguably the best underground journal of the decade, *Arka*, which now is being published officially.

JAN PROKOP (1931–), a poet, translator, fiction writer, essayist, and literary historian, has published, apart from his critical and belletristic prose, just three slim collections of poems, in 1971, 1978, and 1989. He teaches at Jagellonian University in Kraków and the University of Torino in Italy. In the eighties most of his poems and essays were published either underground or abroad.

TADEUSZ RÓŻEWICZ (1921–), a poet, playwright, fiction writer, and essayist, has been a prominent figure in modern Polish literature since his celebrated debut in 1947. His work has been translated into numerous languages, and his plays have been staged throughout the world. His poetry in English translation is available in several selections, including the American edition of his *"The Survivor" and Other Poems* (Princeton University Press), and the British *Conversation with the Prince, and Other Poems* (Anvil Press).

PIOTR SOMMER (1948–), a poet, translator of English and American poetry, and author of children's verse, is an editor of the Warsaw-based monthly *Literatura na świecie* (World Literature). Since his debut in 1977 he has published four books of poems characterized by their ingenious use of colloquial speech. He has also published an anthology of recent British poetry, a collection of interviews with British poets, and a translation of the selected poems of Frank O'Hara.

WISŁAWA SZYMBORSKA (1923–) is the most popular woman poet now living in Poland. She made her debut in 1952 and in subsequent years has published seven more volumes. She has also published translations of French poetry and collections of essays. The poems included here come from her most recent volume, *Ludzie na moście* (The People on the Bridge, 1986), acclaimed as one of the most important collections published in Poland in the 1980s. Her publications in English include *Sounds, Feelings, Thoughts: Seventy Poems by Wisława Szymborska* (Princeton University Press).

JAN TWARDOWSKI (1915–), a priest and rector of a Warsaw church, has long been considered the most original among Polish devotional poets. He published his first collection in 1937, and only resumed publishing his work twenty-two years later. Over the past three decades he has published several highly acclaimed books of poems.

ADAM WAŻYK (1905–81), a poet, fiction writer, playwright, essayist, editor, and translator from Latin, French, and Russian, was a prominent member of the prewar avant-garde and a chief representative of cubism in Polish poetry. He published his first collection in 1924; in the thirties he switched to fiction and only returned to poetry during the war years, which he spent in the Soviet Union. This time, however, he emerged as a representative of Socialist Realism, which he continued to propound after his repatriation, until the unexpected 1955 publication of his highly controversial "Poemat dla dorosłych" ("A Poem for Adults"), a sweeping condemnation of the moral and political failure of People's Poland. In the following years he returned to his old cubist techniques, combining them with present-day thematic concerns. The poems included here come from his last volume, *Zdarzenia* (Occurrences, 1977).

WITOLD WIRPSZA (1918–85) was an innovative poet, playwright, fiction writer, essayist, and translator (chiefly of German literature). He published several Socialist Realist collections between 1949 and 1956, but it was only in the sixties that he emerged as a highly original poet and theoretician of poetry. His collection of essays *Gra znaczeń* (Interplay of Meanings, 1965) provoked a heated debate in literary circles. Although he was primarily concerned with the aesthetics and semiotics of poetry, he did not shun political writing: his book *Pole, wer bist Du?* (Who are you, Pole?), first published in German, earned him repeated attacks from Poland's official media. From 1969 until his death he lived in exile in West Berlin, publishing his books either in the West or through underground presses in Poland. His last poetic collection, *Liturgia* (Liturgy), is actually a complex treatise in verse on the nature of religion.

WIKTOR WOROSZYLSKI (1927–), a prominent poet, translator of Russian poetry, fiction writer, biographer, and essayist, was one of the most ardent supporters of the new political order among the young Polish writers in the late 1940s and early 1950s. Cured by his experiences in the 1956 Budapest uprising, which he covered as a war correspondent, he soon became a leading representative of political dissent in Polish literature. He was a cofounder and editor of the first uncensored literary periodical in Poland, *Zapis*, as well as a participant in many protests and demonstrations. Arrested after the imposition of martial law in 1981, he spent the following year in an internment camp. He has published numerous collections of poems, short stories, and essays, as well as two novels, numerous books for children, and innovative essay biographies of Pushkin, Yesenin, and Mayakovski.

ADAM ZAGAJEWSKI (1945–), a poet, fiction writer, and essayist, is, besides Krynicki, the most prominent representative of the "Generation of '68." He made his debut as a poet in 1972 and has since then published five more books of poems, three novels, and four collections of essays, from the 1974 *The World Not Represented* (in collaboration with Kornhauser) to the recent *Solidarność i samotność* (*Solidarity, Solitude*, Ecco Press). His poems, novels, and essays have been translated into numerous languages. *Tremor*, a collection of his poems in English translation, has been published by Farrar Straus & Giroux. Since 1982 he has lived in France.

INDEX OF FIRST LINES